TEACHER'S EDITION

ON THE
IOWA
TESTS OF
BASIC SKILLS®

LEVEL 12

STECK-VAUGHN
C O M P A N Y
ELEMENTARY • SECONDARY • ADULT • LIBRARY

S0-ALD-082

Acknowledgments

Executive Editor: Diane Sharpe
Project Editor: Janet Jerzycki
Editor: Amanda Johnson
Contributing Author: Jay Comras
Graphics Project Manager: Laura Cole
Graphics Assistant: Sheryl Bankford
Production: Go Media, Inc., Austin, Texas
Cover Design: D Childress/Alan Klemp
Illustrators: Sonya Cohen, Holly Cooper, Julie Gomoll, Gwendolyn Manney,
Rachel Matthews

Pronunciation key reproduced with permission of Macmillan/McGraw-Hill School Publishing Company from *Macmillan School Dictionary 1* (ISBN 0-02-195003-2) *Grade 3–5* and *Macmillan School Dictionary 2* (ISBN 0-02-195004-0) *Grade 6–8*. Copyright © 1990.

Test Best is a registered trademark of Steck-Vaughn Company.

Iowa Tests of Basic Skills is a trademark of The Riverside Publishing Company. Such company has neither endorsed nor authorized this test-preparation book.

Contents

Test Best on the Iowa Tests of Basic Skills has been developed to refresh basic skills, familiarize students with test formats and directions, and to teach test-taking strategies for the Iowa Tests of Basic Skills. *Test Best* provides teachers with materials to ensure that students take the test under optimal conditions—that test-wise students be able to concentrate on what they know without being overwhelmed by a testing situation with which they are unfamiliar.

Being well-prepared for a test means knowing how to approach different types of questions and how to use time wisely. By using the *Test Best* books prior to the administration of the Iowa Tests of Basic Skills, students will learn such skills, as well as be able to control their anxiety about a test and to keep their concentration high throughout the testing period. Armed with the skills they have learned as they work through *Test Best on the Iowa Tests of Basic Skills*, students can truly perform well.

The Steck-Vaughn *Test Best* Series for Grades K–8

Test Best on the Iowa Tests of Basic Skills consists of nine student books. You will need to determine which book is best suited to the abilities and needs of your students. The series is organized as follows:

Book	Grade Levels
Level 5	Kindergarten
Levels 6, 7	Grade 1
Level 8	Grade 2
Level 9	Grade 3
Level 10	Grade 4
Level 11	Grade 5
Level 12	Grade 6
Level 13	Grade 7
Level 14	Grade 8

Objectives of the Series

To Increase Awareness of Test-Taking Strategies

Test-taking strategies should focus on three important test principles:
1. Time Use
   - Not spending too much time on any one question
   - Working rapidly but comfortably
   - Marking items to return to if time permits
   - Using any time remaining to review answers
   - Using a watch (at the appropriate age) to keep track of time
2. Error Avoidance
   - Paying careful attention to directions
   - Determining clearly what is being asked
   - Marking answers in the appropriate place
   - Checking all answers
   - Being neat by avoiding making stray marks on the answer sheet
3. Reasoning
   - Reading the entire question or passage and all the choices before answering a question
   - Applying what has been learned

To Increase Awareness of Directions

It is important that students understand the directions for taking the tests. Therefore, one of the key objectives of the program is to familiarize students with directions. Doing so builds self-confidence and permits students to utilize their time more effectively.

To Increase Awareness of Content and Skills

Anxiety often results from a lack of information about the knowledge and skills the tests will cover. You and your students will find that increased awareness of content and skills are significant outcomes of the program.

To Increase Awareness of Format

By practicing the skills needed to meet your school's educational objectives, the students will be gaining invaluable experience with test formats. Such familiarity permits students to spend more time applying what they have learned.

To Understand How the Test Is Administered

Students are sometimes uncomfortable anticipating what will happen on the day of the tests. Becoming familiar with the procedures, directions, and the process of test taking helps reduce anxiety and uncertainty.

Format of the Books

Each of the nine student books is divided into units that correspond to those found in the Iowa Tests of Basic Skills. The units vary but can include Vocabulary, Word Analysis, Listening, Reading Comprehension, Spelling, Language Mechanics, Language Expression, Math Concepts and Estimation, Math Problems, Math Computation, Maps and Diagrams, and Reference Materials. Within each of these units are the skills covered on the tests. Each skill lesson generally includes:

Directions—clear, concise, and similar to those found in the Iowa Tests of Basic Skills;

Try This— a skill strategy for students that enables them to approach each lesson exercise in a logical manner;

A Sample—to familiarize students with test-taking items;

Think It Through—a specific explanation to students of the correct answer in the Sample item that tells why the incorrect answers are wrong and why the correct answer is correct;

A Practice Section—a set of exercises based on the lesson and modeled on the kinds of exercises found in the Iowa Tests of Basic Skills.

Each unit is followed by a Unit Test that covers all the skills in the unit lessons and affords students the opportunity to experience a situation close to the testing situation. Each book concludes with a series of Comprehensive Tests—one for each unit covered in the book. The *Test Best* Comprehensive tests give students an opportunity to take a test under conditions that parallel those they will face when taking the Iowa Tests of Basic Skills.

The Teacher's Edition

The Teacher's Edition of *Test Best on the Iowa Tests of Basic Skills* contains a Scope and Sequence and reduced student pages complete with answers. The Teacher's Edition also provides a detailed plan of action and suggestions for teaching and administering each of the lessons and tests, including the Sample items. Scripts are provided so that students become familiar with the oral directions given on the tests themselves.

Also contained in the Teacher's Edition is an introductory lesson designed to acquaint students with the *Test Best on the Iowa Tests of Basic Skills* program. This lesson appears on pages 7 through 10 and should be used before beginning Lesson 1 with students.

READING COMPREHENSION SKILLS

Reading Comprehension Skills	Unit 1: Vocabulary	Lesson 1: Matching Words with Similar Meanings	Unit 1 Test	Unit 2: Reading Comprehension	Lesson 2: Reading Selections	Unit 2 Test	COMPREHENSIVE TESTS 1, 2
Identifying words that have similar meanings		■	■		■	■	■
Identifying passage details					■	■	■
Identifying sequence of events					■	■	■
Identifying cause and effect					■	■	■
Understanding a character's traits and motives					■	■	■
Identifying the main idea					■	■	■
Recognizing supporting ideas					■	■	■
Identifying theme					■	■	■
Predicting outcomes					■	■	■
Analyzing author's purpose and effect					■	■	■
Understanding vocabulary		■	■		■	■	■
Distinguishing between fact and opinion					■	■	■
Identifying genre					■	■	■

LANGUAGE SKILLS

Language Skills	Lesson 3: Identifying Word Spellings	Unit 3 Test	Lesson 4: Using Correct Capitalization	Lesson 5: Using Correct Punctuation	Unit 4 Test	Lesson 6: Determining Usage	Lesson 7: Analyzing Paragraphs	Lesson 8: Expressing Ideas Clearly	Lesson 9: Choosing Correct Words and Phrases	Unit 5 Test	COMPREHENSIVE TESTS 3, 4, 5
Identifying correct spellings of words	■	■									■
Recognizing the misspelled word in a phrase	■	■									■
Recognizing errors in capitalization			■	■							■
Identifying correct capitalization in sentences			■	■							■
Recognizing errors in punctuation				■	■						■
Identifying correct punctuation in sentences				■	■						■
Determining the appropriate use of nouns, pronouns, verbs, adjectives, and adverbs in sentences						■			■		■
Determining the topic and supporting details in a paragraph							■			■	■
Identifying information that does not belong in a paragraph							■			■	■
Determining word usage in the context of a paragraph							■			■	■
Identifying sentences that are the clearest, most concise, and best examples of effective writing								■		■	■
Identifying words and phrases that best fit in the context of a sentence									■	■	■

(Column groups: Unit 3: Spelling — Lesson 3, Unit 3 Test; Unit 4: Language Mechanics — Lesson 4, Lesson 5, Unit 4 Test; Unit 5: Language Expression — Lesson 6, Lesson 7, Lesson 8, Lesson 9, Unit 5 Test)

MATHEMATICS SKILLS

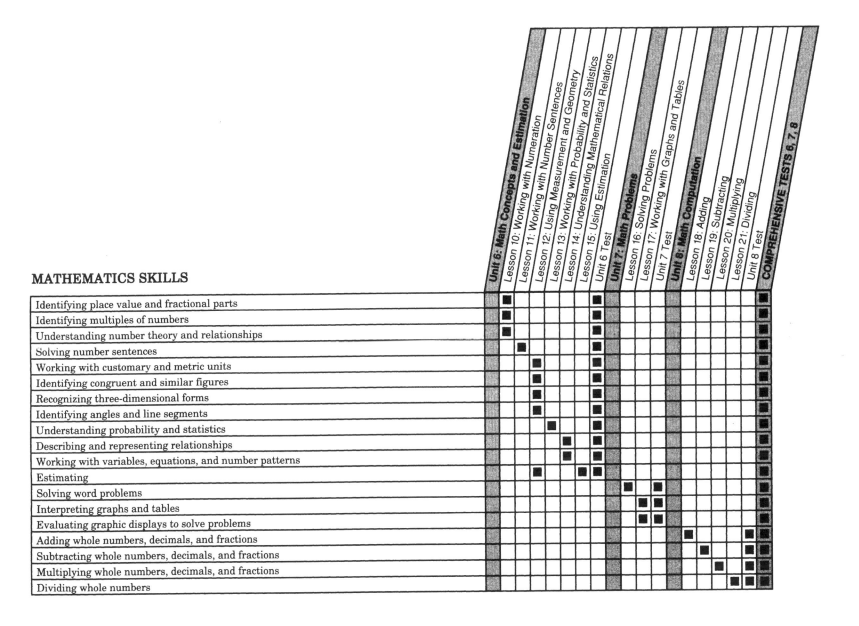

Mathematics Skills	Unit 6: Math Concepts and Estimation	Lesson 10: Working with Numeration	Lesson 11: Working with Number Sentences	Lesson 12: Using Measurement and Geometry	Lesson 13: Working with Probability and Statistics	Lesson 14: Understanding Mathematical Relations	Lesson 15: Using Estimation	Unit 6 Test	Unit 7: Math Problems	Lesson 16: Solving Problems	Lesson 17: Working with Graphs and Tables	Unit 7 Test	Unit 8: Math Computation	Lesson 18: Adding	Lesson 19: Subtracting	Lesson 20: Multiplying	Lesson 21: Dividing	Unit 8 Test	COMPREHENSIVE TESTS 6, 7, 8
Identifying place value and fractional parts		■						■											■
Identifying multiples of numbers		■						■											■
Understanding number theory and relationships		■						■											■
Solving number sentences			■					■											■
Working with customary and metric units				■				■											■
Identifying congruent and similar figures				■				■											■
Recognizing three-dimensional forms				■				■											■
Identifying angles and line segments				■				■											■
Understanding probability and statistics					■			■											■
Describing and representing relationships						■		■											■
Working with variables, equations, and number patterns						■		■											■
Estimating							■	■											■
Solving word problems										■		■							■
Interpreting graphs and tables											■	■							■
Evaluating graphic displays to solve problems											■	■							■
Adding whole numbers, decimals, and fractions														■				■	■
Subtracting whole numbers, decimals, and fractions															■			■	■
Multiplying whole numbers, decimals, and fractions																■		■	■
Dividing whole numbers																	■	■	■

STUDY SKILLS

	Unit 9: Maps and Diagrams	Lesson 22: Working with Maps	Lesson 23: Working with Charts and Diagrams	Unit 9 Test	Unit 10: Reference Materials	Lesson 24: Using an Index	Lesson 25: Using the Dictionary	Lesson 26: Using the Library	Lesson 27: Using Reference Materials	Unit 10 Test	COMPREHENSIVE TESTS 9, 10
Using map symbols and keys to describe and locate places		■		■							■
Determining direction and distance		■		■							■
Interpreting data on population, transportation, elevation, and resources		■		■							■
Tracing travel routes		■		■							■
Interpreting information in schedules, charts, tables, and diagrams			■	■							■
Using an index to locate information						■				■	■
Using alphabetizing skills with dictionary guide words							■			■	■
Obtaining information by interpreting dictionary entries							■			■	■
Choosing appropriate reference materials to gather specific information								■		■	■
Using a card catalog								■		■	■
Identifying key terms to locate appropriate reference materials to find specific information									■	■	■

Introducing Students to *Test Best*

Use this orientation lesson to familiarize students with the format of *Test Best on the Iowa Tests of Basic Skills, Level 12*, and with steps for preparing for and taking the Iowa Tests of Basic Skills.

SAY: **At certain times during the school year, you may take one or more achievement tests. These tests show how well you are doing in certain subjects, compared to other students of your age group across the country.**

Discuss test taking and how students feel about taking standardized tests.

SAY: **Do you remember the last time you took achievement tests? Were you nervous? Were you worried? How did you feel when you finished the tests? Do you think you did your best on the tests?**

Point out to students that most people worry when they have to take a test. Explain that *Test Best* practice lessons and class discussions can help reduce anxiety and help increase confidence.

SAY: **Try not to worry about achievement tests. These tests will not affect your school grades. Instead, the achievement tests will tell you some interesting things about yourself—about the skills you have mastered and the skills you need to learn.**

Distribute the *Test Best* books to students. Tell students that *Test Best* will familiarize them with the kinds of questions on the Iowa Tests of Basic Skills and how it feels to take this kind of test.

SAY: **Some test items will be more difficult than others. Some material may be new to you. But that's all right. You will be given enough time to work on each test.**

Allow students to skim through the books for a minute or two.

SAY: **Now we will look at one of the lessons. Turn to Lesson 1 on page 1. Put your finger on the Directions.**

Explain that each lesson begins with a set of Directions. Ask students why it is important to read and follow directions when taking tests.

UNIT 1 Vocabulary

Lesson 1: Matching Words with Similar Meanings

Directions: Darken the circle for the word or words that mean the <u>same</u> or <u>almost the same</u> as the word in dark type.

| TRY THIS | Read the phrase. Think about the meaning of the boldfaced word. Sometimes you can get a hint about the meaning of the boldfaced word by using the entire phrase. Be careful not to choose a word or words that mean the opposite of the boldfaced word. |

S1 A dull **ache**

  A illness

  B pain

  C wound

  D cut

| THINK IT THROUGH | The correct answer is B. Pain is closest in meaning to <u>ache</u>. Illness, wound, and cut may make sense but do not mean the same as <u>ache</u>. |

STOP

---

1 The **final** chapter
  A last
  B first
  C important
  D most exciting

2 **Capsize** the boat
  J load
  K get out of
  L turn over
  M launch

3 A **frequent** event
  A seldom taking place
  B holiday
  C happening often
  D sad

4 Politely **requested**
  J demanded
  K asked
  L refused
  M answered

5 **Evaluate** the science projects
  A judge
  B honor
  C destroy
  D create

6 A **morsel** of bread
  J small bite
  K fresh loaf
  L large slice
  M spoiled piece

7 To **speculate** about an answer
  A know
  B rely
  C inquire
  D guess

8 The **vertical** flagpole
  J leaning
  K straight up and down
  L straight across
  M broken

9 A winter **festival**
  A celebration
  B journey
  C dessert
  D song

GO ON

Level 12

Answers
S1 Ⓐ ● Ⓒ Ⓓ   2 Ⓙ Ⓚ ● Ⓜ   4 Ⓙ ● Ⓛ Ⓜ   6 ● Ⓚ Ⓛ Ⓜ   8 Ⓙ ● Ⓛ Ⓜ
1 ● Ⓑ Ⓒ Ⓓ   3 Ⓐ Ⓑ ● Ⓓ   5 ● Ⓑ Ⓒ Ⓓ   7 Ⓐ Ⓑ Ⓒ ●   9 ● Ⓑ Ⓒ Ⓓ

1

Lesson 1: Matching Words with Similar Meanings

Directions: Darken the circle for the word or words that mean the same or almost the same as the word in dark type.

TRY THIS	Read the phrase. Think about the meaning of the boldfaced word. Sometimes you can get a hint about the meaning of the boldfaced word by using the entire phrase. Be careful not to choose a word or words that mean the opposite of the boldfaced word.

S1 A dull **ache**

  A illness

  B pain

  C wound

  D cut

THINK IT THROUGH	The correct answer is B. Pain is closest in meaning to ache. Illness, wound, and cut may make sense but do not mean the same as ache.

STOP

1 The **final** chapter

  A last

  B first

  C important

  D most exciting

2 **Capsize** the boat

  J load

  K get out of

  L turn over

  M launch

3 A **frequent** event

  A seldom taking place

  B holiday

  C happening often

  D sad

4 Politely **requested**

  J demanded

  K asked

  L refused

  M answered

5 **Evaluate** the science projects

  A judge

  B honor

  C destroy

  D create

6 A **morsel** of bread

  J small bite

  K fresh loaf

  L large slice

  M spoiled piece

7 To **speculate** about an answer

  A know

  B rely

  C inquire

  D guess

8 The **vertical** flagpole

  J leaning

  K straight up and down

  L straight across

  M broken

9 A winter **festival**

  A celebration

  B journey

  C dessert

  D song

GO ON

Answers

S1 ⒜ ● ⒞ ⒟   2 ⒥ ⒦ ● ⓜ   4 ⒥ ● ⒧ ⓜ   6 ● ⒦ ⒧ ⓜ   8 ⒥ ● ⒧ ⓜ

1 ● ⒝ ⒞ ⒟   3 ⒜ ⒝ ● ⒟   5 ● ⒝ ⒞ ⒟   7 ⒜ ⒝ ⒞ ●   9 ● ⒝ ⒞ ⒟

Level 12

1

SAY: **Find the Try This section. Let's read this section together. Try This suggests a way to answer the question. There are other ways to figure the answer to a question. Try This offers one way. Now look at the Sample below Try This. We will always work through the Samples together before you work the practice exercises on your own.**

Copy the Sample onto the chalkboard. Work through the Sample orally with students, and demonstrate the proper way to darken the answer spaces. Explain to students the importance of filling the answer space, pressing firmly on the pencil to make a dark mark, and erasing any stray marks that might be picked up as answers by the scoring machines.

SAY: **Now find Think It Through. Think It Through is an explanation of the best answer. Think It Through usually explains why the other choices are wrong.**

Ask students if they have any questions about the lesson features up to this point.

SAY: **What do you see below Think It Through? (The word STOP) What should you do when you see the word STOP? (Stop what you are doing.)**

Tell students that they will see the word STOP throughout the lessons and on the Iowa Tests of Basic Skills. Explain that the word STOP tells students to stop what they are doing, put their pencils down, and wait for further instructions from the teacher.

SAY: **What do you see below Think It Through and the word STOP? (Numbered exercises) Each lesson has a practice section with exercises.**

What do you see at the bottom of page 1? (The words GO ON) These words tell you to turn to the next page and continue working.

Explain to students that the words GO ON will appear in some two-page lessons, in the unit tests, and in the comprehensive tests.

Unit 1 Test

S1 **Lighten** the load
  A make smaller
  B turn over
  C turn on
  D destroy

STOP

For questions 1–13, darken the circle for the word or words that mean the <u>same</u> or <u>almost the same</u> as the word in dark type.

1 A **rise** in the temperature
  A change
  B mistake
  C decrease
  D increase

2 **Observe** the traffic signs
  J paint
  K open
  L dismiss
  M obey

3 **Overcome** your fear
  A give in to
  B conquer
  C recognize
  D ignore

4 A **wrinkled** jacket
  J dirty
  K closed
  L silk
  M creased

5 **Accumulate** a fortune
  A pile up
  B give away
  C accept
  D steal

6 A **courageous** person
  J friendly
  K brave
  L confused
  M active

7 A **defective** part
  A perfect
  B intact
  C whole
  D broken

8 **Descend** the stairs
  J go up
  K go down
  L scrub
  M varnish

9 A **clump** of clover
  A forest
  B meadow
  C field
  D bunch

10 **Drenched** in the rain
  J drained
  K soaked
  L lost
  M dripped

11 A **tragic** mistake
  A very sad
  B common
  C very funny
  D rare

12 A thief's **accomplice**
  J neighbor
  K loot
  L helper
  M arrest

13 **Knead** the dough
  A add water to
  B mix
  C secure
  D bake

STOP

Answers
S1 ● Ⓑ Ⓒ Ⓓ   3 Ⓐ ● Ⓒ Ⓓ   6 Ⓙ ● Ⓛ Ⓜ   9 Ⓐ Ⓑ Ⓒ ●   12 Ⓙ Ⓚ ● Ⓜ   Level 12
1 Ⓐ Ⓑ Ⓒ ●   4 Ⓙ Ⓚ Ⓛ ●   7 Ⓐ Ⓑ Ⓒ ●   10 Ⓙ ● Ⓛ Ⓜ   13 Ⓐ ● Ⓒ Ⓓ
2 Ⓙ Ⓚ Ⓛ ●   5 ● Ⓑ Ⓒ Ⓓ   8 Ⓙ ● Ⓛ Ⓜ   11 ● Ⓑ Ⓒ Ⓓ   **3**

Have students turn to the Unit 1 Test on page 3. Explain that there is a unit test at the end of each unit that gives students an opportunity to practice taking a test. Have students locate the <u>Sample</u> at the beginning of the test. Tell students that you will always work the <u>Sample</u> together as a class before they work the rest of the test. Explain that this test will include the skills practiced in the unit lessons.

Ask students if they have any questions about the lessons or the unit tests.

Comprehensive Tests
Test 1: Vocabulary

S1 Accept a gift
   A give
   B receive
   C buy
   D sell

STOP

For questions 1–28, darken the circle for the word or words that mean the <u>same</u> or <u>almost the same</u> as the word in <u>dark type</u>.

1 A **bare** cupboard
   A empty
   B clean
   C dirty
   D full

2 A **colossal** statue
   J marble
   K broken
   L ordinary
   M huge

3 **Employ** an assistant
   A hire
   B want
   C replace
   D purchase

4 **Demonstrate** the new computer
   J adjust
   K turn off
   L show
   M package

5 **Bind** the packages
   A open
   B send
   C receive
   D secure

6 The **core** of the earth
   J crust
   K center
   L atmosphere
   M axis

7 To **incline** toward
   A lean
   B invade
   C support
   D vary

8 A **notorious** spy
   J bothersome
   K destructive
   L well-known
   M beginning

9 Disobey the **ordinance**
   A law
   B conference
   C parent
   D judge

10 **Prune** the fruit tree
   J plant
   K throw out
   L trim
   M light

11 An **expensive** car
   A costly
   B foreign
   C excellent
   D fast

12 An **actual** fort
   J acute
   K ancient
   L real
   M strong

13 A **spare** tire
   A extra
   B rubber
   C flat
   D worn

GO ON

Explain that (at the end of the book) there are Comprehensive Tests.

SAY: **Turn to page 65. Read the title at the top of the page.** (*Comprehensive Tests, Test 1: Vocabulary*) **There are ten Comprehensive Tests—one test for each unit in the book. When we take the Comprehensive Tests, we will follow the test conditions that will be used during the Iowa Tests of Basic Skills. For example, I will provide you with sharpened pencils and scratch paper for the mathematics tests. Also, each test will have a time limit. The Comprehensive Tests will give you a final chance to apply the skills that you practiced in the lessons in** *Test Best* **before you take the Iowa Tests of Basic Skills.**

Ask students if they have any questions about the Comprehensive Tests.

SAY: **When you take the Iowa Tests of Basic Skills, you may feel a little nervous at first. Try to remember what you have learned in** *Test Best* **about taking tests. You will be able to use what you have learned in your classes, too. Then you should be ready to do your very best.**

UNIT 1 Vocabulary

Lesson 1: Matching Words with Similar Meanings

Directions: Darken the circle for the word or words that mean the <u>same</u> or <u>almost the same</u> as the word in dark type.

TRY THIS

Read the phrase. Think about the meaning of the boldfaced word. Sometimes you can get a hint about the meaning of the boldfaced word by using the entire phrase. Be careful not to choose a word or words that mean the opposite of the boldfaced word.

S1 A dull **ache**
A illness
B pain
C wound
D cut

THINK IT THROUGH

The correct answer is B. Pain is closest in meaning to ache. Illness, wound, and cut may make sense but do not mean the same as ache.

STOP

1 The **final** chapter
A last
B first
C important
D most exciting

2 **Capsize** the boat
J load
K get out of
L turn over
M launch

3 A **frequent** event
A seldom taking place
B holiday
C happening often
D sad

4 Politely **requested**
J demanded
K asked
L refused
M answered

5 **Evaluate** the science projects
A judge
B honor
C destroy
D create

6 A **morsel** of bread
J small bite
K fresh loaf
L large slice
M spoiled piece

7 To **speculate** about an answer
A know
B rely
C inquire
D guess

8 The **vertical** flagpole
J leaning
K straight up and down
L straight across
M broken

9 A winter **festival**
A celebration
B journey
C dessert
D song

GO ON

Level 12

Answers
S1 Ⓐ ● Ⓒ Ⓓ   2 Ⓙ Ⓚ ● Ⓜ   4 Ⓙ ● Ⓛ Ⓜ   6 ● Ⓚ Ⓛ Ⓜ   8 Ⓙ ● Ⓛ Ⓜ
1 ● Ⓑ Ⓒ Ⓓ   3 Ⓐ Ⓑ ● Ⓓ   5 ● Ⓑ Ⓒ Ⓓ   7 Ⓐ Ⓑ Ⓒ ●   9 ● Ⓑ Ⓒ Ⓓ

1

UNIT 1 Vocabulary

Lesson 1: Matching Words with Similar Meanings

Reading Skill: Identifying words that have similar meanings

SAY: **Turn to Lesson 1, Matching Words with Similar Meanings, on page 1.**

Check to see that all students find Lesson 1.

SAY: **In Lesson 1 you will practice matching words that have similar meanings.**

Read the <u>Directions</u> to students.

SAY: **Now look at <u>Try This</u>.**

Read <u>Try This</u> to students.

SAY: **Now look at S1. Read the phrase and the answer choices carefully. Then darken the circle for the word that has the same or almost the same meaning as the word in dark type, *ache*.**

Allow students time to find and mark their answer.

SAY: **Now look at <u>Think It Through</u>.**

Read <u>Think It Through</u> to students. Check to see that all students have filled in the correct answer space. Ask students if they have any questions.

SAY: **Now you will practice matching more words with similar meanings. Do numbers 1 through 24 just as we did S1. When you come to the words *GO ON* at the bottom of page 1, continue working on the next page. When you come to the word *STOP* at the bottom of page 2, put your pencils down. You may now begin.**

Allow students time to find and mark their answers.

10 **Gauge** the distance
J cover
K increase
L decrease
M measure

11 A **dingy** room
A damp
B dirty-looking
C clammy
D newly planted

12 A brightly colored **banner**
J scarf
K flag
L seal
M ship

13 **Admit** your mistake
A confess
B hide
C change
D improve

14 A **dense** fog
J thick
K smoky
L dirty
M dangerous

15 **Cushion** the fall
A hasten
B soften
C expect
D prevent

16 A **brief** talk
J short
K boring
L serious
M loud

17 The building **collapsed**
A fell down
B went up
C sold out
D blew up

18 **Flee** the city
J enter into
K clean
L rebuild
M run away from

19 The **vacant** seat
A lumpy
B uncomfortable
C empty
D lopsided

20 **Depress** the button
J twist
K turn
L pull out
M push down

21 His **customary** seat
A usual
B cushioned
C useful
D comfortable

22 A **hint** of danger
J time
K day
L slight sign
M mission

23 **Liberate** the country
A transfer
B free
C honor
D protect

24 A **brisk** pace
J slow
K steady
L quick
M musical

STOP

Level 12

Answers

10 Ⓙ Ⓚ Ⓛ ●   13 ● Ⓑ Ⓒ Ⓓ   16 ● Ⓚ Ⓛ Ⓜ   19 Ⓐ Ⓑ ● Ⓓ   22 Ⓙ Ⓚ ● Ⓜ
11 Ⓐ ● Ⓒ Ⓓ   14 ● Ⓚ Ⓛ Ⓜ   17 ● Ⓑ Ⓒ Ⓓ   20 Ⓙ Ⓚ Ⓛ ●   23 Ⓐ ● Ⓒ Ⓓ
12 Ⓙ ● Ⓛ Ⓜ   15 Ⓐ ● Ⓒ Ⓓ   18 Ⓙ Ⓚ Ⓛ ●   21 ● Ⓑ Ⓒ Ⓓ   24 Ⓙ Ⓚ ● Ⓜ

2

Unit 1 Test

S1 Lighten the load
- A make smaller
- B turn over
- C turn on
- D destroy

—————— **STOP**

For questions 1–13, darken the circle for the word or words that mean the same or almost the same as the word in dark type.

1 A rise in the temperature
- A change
- B mistake
- C decrease
- D increase

2 Observe the traffic signs
- J paint
- K open
- L dismiss
- M obey

3 Overcome your fear
- A give in to
- B conquer
- C recognize
- D ignore

4 A wrinkled jacket
- J dirty
- K closed
- L silk
- M creased

5 Accumulate a fortune
- A pile up
- B give away
- C accept
- D steal

6 A courageous person
- J friendly
- K brave
- L confused
- M active

7 A defective part
- A perfect
- B intact
- C whole
- D broken

8 Descend the stairs
- J go up
- K go down
- L scrub
- M varnish

9 A clump of clover
- A forest
- B meadow
- C field
- D bunch

10 Drenched in the rain
- J drained
- K soaked
- L lost
- M dripped

11 A tragic mistake
- A very sad
- B common
- C very funny
- D rare

12 A thief's accomplice
- J neighbor
- K loot
- L helper
- M arrest

13 Knead the dough
- A add water to
- B mix
- C secure
- D bake

—————— **STOP**

Answers
S1 ● Ⓑ Ⓒ Ⓓ   3 Ⓐ ● Ⓒ Ⓓ   6 Ⓙ ● Ⓛ Ⓜ   9 Ⓐ Ⓑ Ⓒ ●   12 Ⓙ Ⓚ ● Ⓜ   Level 12
1 Ⓐ Ⓑ Ⓒ ●   4 Ⓙ Ⓚ Ⓛ ●   7 Ⓐ Ⓑ Ⓒ ●   10 Ⓙ ● Ⓛ Ⓜ   13 Ⓐ ● Ⓒ Ⓓ
2 Ⓙ Ⓚ Ⓛ ●   5 ● Ⓑ Ⓒ Ⓓ   8 Ⓙ ● Ⓛ Ⓜ   11 ● Ⓑ Ⓒ Ⓓ   **3**

Unit 1 Test

SAY: **Turn to the Unit 1 Test on page 3.**

Check to see that all students find the Unit 1 Test.

SAY: **In this test you will use the language skills that we have practiced in this unit. Now look at S1. Which word has the same or almost the same meaning as the word in dark type? Darken the circle for the correct answer.**

Allow students time to find and mark their answer.

SAY: **You should have darkened the circle for A. Make smaller are the words closest in meaning to the word in dark type, Lighten.**

Check to see that all students have filled in the correct answer space. Ask students if they have any questions.

SAY: **Now you will finish the test on your own. Read the directions carefully. Do numbers 1 through 13 just as we did S1. Read the phrases and answer choices carefully. Then darken the circle for each correct answer. When you come to the word STOP at the bottom of page 3, put your pencils down. You may now begin.**

Allow students time to find and mark their answers.

SAY: **It is now time to stop. You have completed the Unit 1 Test. Make sure that you have carefully filled in your answer spaces and have completely erased any stray marks. Then put your pencils down.**

After the test has been scored, review the questions and answer choices with students. If students are having difficulty, provide them with additional practice items.

UNIT 2 Reading Comprehension

Lesson 2: Reading Selections

Directions: Carefully read each story and the questions that follow. Darken the circle for the correct answer.

> **TRY THIS** More than one answer choice may sound correct. Choose the answer that goes best with the story.

S1 Sylvia's first day of school was difficult. She had just moved from another state. Sylvia felt lonely and scared as she tried to find her classrooms. Nothing seemed to go right that day.

Which word best describes Sylvia's feelings about the first day at her new school?

A Unhappy

B Joyful

C Confident

D Angry

> **THINK IT THROUGH** The correct answer is A. This was Sylvia's first day at a new school. The third sentence states that Sylvia was lonely and scared. The word <u>unhappy</u> best describes those feelings.

STOP

Racing, Sweating
Bouncing, Jamming
Passing, Catching
Shooting, Dunking
Swishing, Jumping

All these actions make my body sore.
But I love to hear the crowd roar.
The noise lifts me out of my seat.
My ears hurt, though, when there's a defeat,
From the silence that bounces off the walls.
I go home reviewing the ref's calls.
I look forward to the next game.
They are always different, never the same.

1 What sport does this poem describe?

A Ice hockey

B Basketball

C Baseball

D Downhill skiing

2 According to the poem, what makes the poet's "ears hurt"?

J The roar of the crowd

K The noise from bouncing

L The jumping out of the seat

M The silence that bounces off the walls

3 Which of the following best describes the tone of the poem?

A Jealousy   C Liveliness

B Sadness   D Boredom

GO ON

Level 12

Answers

S1 ● Ⓑ Ⓒ Ⓓ   2 Ⓙ Ⓚ Ⓛ ●

1 Ⓐ ● Ⓒ Ⓓ   3 Ⓐ Ⓑ ● Ⓓ

4

UNIT 2 Reading Comprehension

Lesson 2: Reading Selections

Reading Skills: Identifying passage details, sequence of events, cause and effect; understanding a character's traits and motives; identifying the main idea; recognizing supporting ideas; identifying theme; predicting outcomes; analyzing author's purpose and effect; understanding vocabulary; distinguishing between fact and opinion; identifying genre

SAY: **Turn to Lesson 2, Reading Selections, on page 4.**

Check to see that all students find Lesson 2.

SAY: **In Lesson 2 you will practice answering questions about selections that you read.**

Read the <u>Directions</u> to students.

SAY: **Now look at <u>Try This</u>.**

Read <u>Try This</u> to students.

SAY: **Now look at S1. Read the selection. Then answer the question that follows. Which word best describes Sylvia's feelings about the first day at her new school? Darken the circle for the correct answer.**

Allow students time to find and mark their answer.

SAY: **Now look at <u>Think It Through</u>.**

Read <u>Think It Through</u> to students. Check to see that all students have filled in the correct answer space. Ask students if they have any questions.

SAY: **Now you will practice answering more questions about selections that you read. Read each selection carefully and answer the questions that follow. Do numbers 1 through 24 just as we did S1. When you come to the words *GO ON* at the bottom of a page, continue working on the next page. When you come to the word *STOP* at the bottom of page 8, put your pencils down. You may now begin.**

Allow students time to find and mark their answers.

> Dear Sheriff,
>
> I saw you and your men capture Robin Hood in Sherwood Forest the other night. The charges of theft that you have brought against Robin are ridiculous. He is no more a criminal than is Maid Marian. Robin has an alibi. Will Scarlett and I were with him on the evening of the alleged robbery. We were hunting, and I have the game that we caught to prove it.
>
> You, sir, are the one who should be in jail. You are a corrupt, selfish man. You force poor people to work long hours on your land for little pay. Then you have the nerve to charge them taxes for your "protection" from harm. You are the true thief.
>
> If you do not release Robin Hood within the next 24 hours, I will lead a band of his followers to the jail where he is being held. We will force your men to release him.
>
> Sincerely,
> Little John

4 According to the selection, who did the sheriff and his men capture in Sherwood Forest?

J Little John

K Maid Marian

L Will Scarlett

M Robin Hood

5 In the first paragraph, "alibi" means

A a confession of guilt for committing a crime.

B a story that teaches a lesson.

C proof of having been somewhere else when a crime was committed.

D a twin brother or sister.

6 In this selection, "game" refers to

J animals hunted for food.

K a plan of action.

L hunting arrows.

M a contest.

7 What does "corrupt" mean in the second paragraph?

A Hard-working

B Dishonest

C Powerful

D Wealthy

8 According to Little John, who is the thief?

J The sheriff of Nottingham

K Robin Hood

L Will Scarlett

M Maid Marian

9 This letter would most likely appear in a book of

A biographies.

B legends.

C nonfiction stories.

D science.

GO ON

Answers

4 Ⓙ Ⓚ Ⓛ ● 6 ● Ⓚ Ⓛ Ⓜ 8 ● Ⓚ Ⓛ Ⓜ

5 Ⓐ Ⓑ ● Ⓓ 7 Ⓐ ● Ⓒ Ⓓ 9 Ⓐ ● Ⓒ Ⓓ

Do you suffer from allergies? Did you know that more than 40 million people in the United States have allergy problems? You may have heard the word *allergy* many times without knowing exactly what it means. An allergy is an unusual reaction to something that is harmless to most people. For example, if you have a ragweed allergy, you probably start sneezing whenever you're near ragweed. If you have a shellfish allergy, you might develop a rash if you eat lobster, shrimp, or crawfish.

Throughout time people probably have had allergies. The pictographs on the tomb wall of an Egyptian king show that he died after being stung by a bee. This was a violent allergic reaction. Around A.D. 200 a Greek physician wrote about people sneezing when they were exposed to certain plants. Although allergies have existed for thousands of years, it was not until the middle 1800s that the medical community began to understand the causes and characteristics of allergies. At that time an English physician, W.R. Kirkman, collected the yellow dust called pollen from grasses he had grown. When he began to sneeze, he realized that he had discovered the cause of hay fever.

About the same time, another English doctor, Charles Blackley, developed an allergy test. He scratched one of his arms and put rye grass pollen on the cut. The scratch itched, turned red, and swelled. Blackley then scratched his other arm without adding pollen to the cut. Nothing happened. Blackley had the proof that he was allergic to rye grass. This test is called a scratch test, and it is still used today.

Our bodies protect us from germs and viruses by making substances called antibodies. Antibodies fight the germs and viruses that cause illness. An allergic reaction is really a mistake—the body mistakes something that is usually harmless, such as pollen, for a harmful invader. Special antibodies are produced, and then the body releases a chemical that causes a runny nose, itchy skin, and sometimes wheezing.

The material that produces an allergic reaction is called an allergen. Many allergens, such as mold, pollen, and mites, are present in the air. Mold is a small plant that grows in wet places. Mold seeds are carried by the wind. Many grasses, weeds, and trees produce pollen that is carried by the wind. Mites are insects that are so small they cannot be seen. If you sneeze when the wind blows, you may be allergic to one of these things.

People can be allergic to many different things. Some people are allergic to certain foods. Allergic reactions to these foods often include an upset stomach, hives, or breathing problems. Some foods that cause allergic reactions are dairy products, wheat, corn, nuts, seafood, eggs, chocolate, and oranges.

Some people are allergic to drugs, such as aspirin and penicillin, and other people are allergic to certain chemicals present in soaps and paints. Some people have allergic reactions when they are stung by bees, ants, or mosquitoes. Doctors can help the allergy sufferer by prescribing pills, sprays, or nose drops. If these are ineffective, doctors sometimes suggest allergy shots.

10 How do we know that people had allergies thousands of years ago?

J Scientists have found ragweed fossils.

K Scientists found cave drawings that show people sneezing.

L The records of doctors living thousands of years ago tell about allergies.

M Pictures on the tomb of an Egyptian king show that he died after being stung by a bee.

11 If you have hay fever, you should

A avoid fields when grasses are producing pollen.

B use special soap to avoid a rash.

C produce allergens.

D avoid eating any dairy products.

12 What is the main idea of paragraph 3?

J Blackley was allergic to rye grass.

K Blackley invented the scratch test to learn whether a person has an allergy.

L Blackley scratched both of his arms, but only one itched, reddened, and swelled.

M Blackley was an English doctor.

13 What does the word "antibodies" mean in paragraph 4?

A Germs blown in the wind

B Viruses that attack the body

C Substances that the body makes to fight illness

D Medicine given to allergy sufferers

14 In an allergic reaction, the body mistakes an allergen for

J pollen.

K an antibody.

L a blood cell.

M a harmful invader.

15 If you sneeze when the wind blows, you may be allergic to

A penicillin.

B mold, pollen, or mites.

C shellfish.

D bees.

16 Some people are allergic to

J rice.

K tea.

L dairy products.

M meat.

17 The author of this selection probably wrote it to

A describe allergy research in the 1800's.

B inform readers about allergies.

C persuade readers to get allergy shots.

D show readers that allergies are painful.

18 The word "material" in paragraph 5 means

J fabric.

K relevant.

L expensive.

M substance.

19 Where would this selection be most likely to appear?

A In a history of Greece

B In a science textbook

C In a magazine

D In an encyclopedia

GO ON

Level 12

Answers

10 Ⓙ Ⓚ Ⓛ ●   12 Ⓙ ● Ⓛ Ⓜ   14 Ⓙ Ⓚ Ⓛ ●   16 Ⓙ Ⓚ ● Ⓜ   18 Ⓙ Ⓚ Ⓛ ●

11 ● Ⓑ Ⓒ Ⓓ   13 Ⓐ Ⓑ ● Ⓓ   15 Ⓐ ● Ⓒ Ⓓ   17 Ⓐ ● Ⓒ Ⓓ   19 Ⓐ Ⓑ ● Ⓓ

7

The other day while my family and I were stuck in our car in a traffic jam, my brother Jerry started to draw what he called the "future vehicle." It was the most unusual vehicle I had ever seen.

We had just heard a siren. It was an ambulance trying to make its way through the thick traffic jam on the highway. It had to zigzag through the slow-moving automobiles.

"You see, that's the problem with ambulances. They are too wide to easily navigate through heavy traffic. They should be elongated and thinner. Then they could fit between lanes of traffic. Look at my idea of an ambulance," said Jerry pointing to his unearthly drawing.

As traffic began to flow smoothly, Jerry continued to explain how his version of an ambulance would work. It was beginning to make sense to me. Dad said it was a great idea. Mom suggested that Jerry get a patent for his invention to make sure his idea was not stolen.

Jerry was excited and decided to find out how to get a patent. He learned that before you try to patent your idea, you must make sure that no one has a similar patent already. Some people hire an agent to check this for them. The agent checks with the U.S. Patent and Trademark Office, which has millions of patents registered. The agent must also check foreign patents. After the search, Jerry would have to fill out an application and include drawings and a description of his new vehicle. It could take as long as two years for the patent to be granted.

If Jerry receives his patent, he will be given a patent number that tells the date of the invention. Jerry will have certain rights as an inventor. No one other than the inventor can make or sell the patented item for 17 years.

Learning about patents was an interesting experience. Jerry learned that he is not the only one with an unusual invention. I hope his idea is successful and that it does not become just another number on the shelf in the U.S. Patent and Trademark Office in Arlington, Virginia.

20 Why does Jerry think ambulances should be thinner?

J They could be seen more easily.

K They could fit between traffic lanes.

L They could move more quickly.

M They would prevent traffic jams.

21 What does the word "elongated" mean in paragraph 3?

A Broken into parts

B Lengthened

C Removed

D Trimmed

22 Which of the following is a step in obtaining a patent?

J The inventor must write to a company to sell his or her idea.

K An agent must verify the date of the invention.

L The inventor must verify that there is no similar patent listed.

M An agent must be hired to work for the inventor.

23 An application for a patent must include

A a $200 fee.

B a working model of the invention.

C drawings and a description of the invention.

D a parent's or guardian's signature if the applicant is under 18 years of age.

24 What conclusion can be drawn from the last sentence of the passage?

J A patent number ensures the success of the invention.

K The U.S. Patent and Trademark Office is very old.

L Jerry's invention is unusual.

M Not all inventions are successes.

STOP

Level 12

Answers

8

20 Ⓙ ● Ⓛ Ⓜ   22 Ⓙ Ⓚ ● Ⓜ   24 Ⓙ Ⓚ Ⓛ ●

21 Ⓐ ● Ⓒ Ⓓ   23 Ⓐ Ⓑ ● Ⓓ

S1   Erin needed to read a fantasy book to fulfill a reading requirement. She asked a librarian to help her select a book. The librarian suggested *The Lion, the Witch, and the Wardrobe* by C. S. Lewis. Erin explained that she had already read all books written by C. S. Lewis.

What probably happened next?

A Erin checked out *The Lion, the Witch, and the Wardrobe.*

B The librarian suggested another fantasy book to Erin.

C Erin thanked the librarian and went home.

D The librarian told Erin that she should go to another library to find a book.

STOP

For questions 1–19, darken the circle for the correct answer.

Dear Jack,

I have to work a little later than I expected today. Would you please make dinner? I've left a copy of Simple Gourmet Cooking *on the kitchen counter. How about making the Super Taco Salad on page 211? It's nutritious, filling, and delicious. For dessert you'll find some packages of gelatin in the pantry. Gelatin tastes good with fruit mixed into it. You should find some fruit in the refrigerator.*

I'd also appreciate it if you would wash the breakfast dishes and water the plants— those inside the house and the ones on the front porch.

I'll see you around six o'clock. Thanks for your help, and have fun cooking.

Love,
Mom

---

1   What is the main purpose of this letter?

A To explain how to make a "Super Taco Salad"

B To explain why Mom is going to be late

C To explain which plants to water

D To explain what chores Jack should do before Mom gets home

2   Jack made the salad and the gelatin. He also washed the dishes. He was asked to do one more thing before his mother arrives home. **What was it?**

J Water the plants

K Mop the floor

L Feed the dog

M Go to the store

3   What did Jack's mother suggest that he add to the gelatin?

A Ice cubes

B Fruit

C Juice

D Sugar

4   What is the meaning of the word "nutritious" in the first paragraph?

J Tasty

K Inedible

L Spicy

M Healthful

GO ON

Level 12

Answers
S1 ⓐ ● ⓒ ⓓ   2 ● ⓚ ⓛ ⓜ   4 ⓙ ⓚ ⓛ ●
1 ⓐ ⓑ ⓒ ●   3 ⓐ ● ⓒ ⓓ

9

Unit 2 Test

SAY: **Turn to the Unit 2 Test on page 9.**

Check to see that all students find the Unit 2 Test.

SAY: **In this test you will use the reading skills that we have practiced in this unit. Look at S1. Read the selection. Then answer the question that follows. What probably happened next? Darken the circle for the correct answer.**

Allow students time to find and mark their answers.

SAY: **You should have darkened the circle for *B* because Erin wanted to read any fantasy book, not specifically one by C.S. Lewis.**

Check to see that all students have filled in the correct answer space. Ask students if they have any questions.

SAY: **Now you will finish the test on your own. Carefully read each selection and the questions that follow. Do numbers 1 through 19 just as we did S1. Darken the circle for each correct answer. When you come to the words *GO ON* at the bottom of a page, continue working on the next page. When you come to the word *STOP* at the bottom of page 12, put your pencils down. You may now begin.**

Allow students time to find and mark their answers.

The California Gold Rush of 1848 began at John Sutter's sawmill in the Sacramento Valley. Sutter was a shopkeeper from Switzerland. He had come to California ten years before, hoping to find a new life. He probably never dreamed that gold would be found on his land.

One day one of Mr. Sutter's partners, John Marshall, found a shiny nugget in a ditch near the sawmill. It was the size of a dime. Marshall tested the nugget to see if it was in fact the precious metal, gold. He tried shattering it and tarnishing it. He put it in lye to see if it would melt or crack. It did none of these things. Marshall was very excited and rode all one night to show the nugget to Sutter. Sutter was skeptical at first. He couldn't believe that there might be gold on his land. Then he tried the ultimate test. He poured nitric acid on the metal to see if it would be eaten away. It was not.

When news of the discovery broke, California was changed forever. Sutter and Marshall could no longer operate the sawmill. Their workers abandoned their jobs to search for gold. People from all over the country came to California. Even people from Europe and China arrived in California to look for gold.

New trails were opened to the West. No one seemed to mind the hardships of pioneer living as long as they found gold. In 1848 the population of California grew from 20,000 to 107,000 people. San Francisco and Sacramento were transformed from sleepy towns into booming cities. Miners who found gold were eager to spend their money in the cities. Others who were not so lucky remained in the area and became farmers or ranchers. The Gold Rush lasted from 1848 until 1852. During that time the population continued to grow, and in 1850 California became a state.

Unfortunately, the Gold Rush was not very good for Sutter and Marshall. So many people were living on the land around the sawmill that Sutter was forced to give up his claim to the land. Marshall tried searching for gold but never had much luck after his initial find.

GO ON

5 What is the main topic of this selection?

A John Sutter's sawmill

B The life of John Marshall

C The history of Sacramento

D The Gold Rush

6 Which word best describes California during the Gold Rush?

J Uneventful

K Pessimistic

L Prosperous

M Frightening

7 Why is gold considered a precious metal?

A It is easily tarnished, and lye melts it.

B It is very valuable.

C People use it to make chains and other jewelry.

D It is used only to make coins.

8 What does the word "skeptical" mean in paragraph 2?

J Doubtful

K Hopeful

L Inspired

M Puzzled

9 Why did so many people leave their homes and jobs to search for gold?

A They wanted to see California.

B They wanted to experience pioneer living.

C They hoped to become rich quickly.

D They hated their jobs.

10 Why did John Sutter come to California?

J He wanted to search for gold.

K He wanted a new life.

L He found a job as a shopkeeper in Sacramento.

M He had inherited a ranch in California from a relative.

11 What are paragraphs 3 and 4 mainly about?

A How California became a state

B How the Gold Rush affected California

C How people lived in California during the Gold Rush

D How gold was discovered in California

12 What was the author's purpose in writing this passage?

J To describe the beauties of gold

K To convince the reader that gold is important

L To tell the history of the California Gold Rush

M To advertise gold jewelry

13 Which of the following events happened first?

A The population of California grew.

B Trails were open to the West.

C Marshall discovered gold near the sawmill.

D California became a state.

GO ON

Answers

5 Ⓐ Ⓑ Ⓒ ●   7 Ⓐ ● Ⓒ Ⓓ   9 Ⓐ Ⓑ ● Ⓓ   11 Ⓐ ● Ⓒ Ⓓ   13 Ⓐ Ⓑ ● Ⓓ

6 Ⓙ Ⓚ ● Ⓜ   8 ● Ⓚ Ⓛ Ⓜ   10 Ⓙ ● Ⓛ Ⓜ   12 Ⓙ Ⓚ ● Ⓜ

When Christine read the flier in the library about the baby-sitting class, she went directly to the librarian. "I would like to register for the baby-sitting class," Christine told the librarian. "I want to earn money to go to summer camp. Perhaps I can get more baby-sitting jobs if I take this class."

According to the flier, the baby-sitting class would teach the students important skills such as infant care, games to play with toddlers, and first aid. The flier also promised that participants would learn how to find baby-sitting jobs. The class would meet every Tuesday evening for five weeks.

Christine attended all the classes. She felt that she would be a much better baby-sitter as a result of her new skills. Christine especially enjoyed learning about infant care. On the other hand, she felt that the hardest lesson was about first aid. She felt confident that she could handle an emergency, but she hoped the need to use her first-aid skills never occurred.

The library awarded certificates of achievement to participants who passed the final test. Christine used her certificate to advertise for baby-sitting jobs. Her advertisement showed her certificate and listed her phone number, her hourly rates, and the days she was available. Then she passed the advertisement out to everyone she knew who might use her services.

14 Where did Christine learn about the baby-sitting class?

J At summer camp

K In the library

L At a friend's house

M In a newspaper ad

15 According to the flier, the baby-sitting class would meet

A once.

B three times.

C five times.

D ten times.

16 Why did Christine want to earn money?

J To pay for a baby-sitting class

K To buy clothes for summer

L To pay for summer camp

M To pay for school expenses

17 According to the selection, which of the following was a skill taught in the class?

A Meal preparation

B First aid

C Discipline

D Housekeeping

18 Which word best describes Christine's attitude toward the class?

J Enthusiastic

K Indifferent

L Bitter

M Hesitant

19 The main idea of the last paragraph helps the reader to conclude that Christine

A turned down baby-sitting offers.

B was anxious to baby-sit.

C went to the library on a daily basis.

D failed to complete the baby-sitting class.

STOP

Level 12

Answers

12

14 ⓙ ● ⓛ ⓜ   16 ⓙ ⓚ ● ⓜ   18 ● ⓚ ⓛ ⓜ

15 Ⓐ Ⓑ ● Ⓓ   17 Ⓐ ● Ⓒ Ⓓ   19 Ⓐ ● Ⓒ Ⓓ

SAY: **It is now time to stop. You have completed the Unit 2 Test. Make sure that you have carefully filled in your answer spaces and have completely erased any stray marks. Then put your pencils down.**

After the test has been scored, review the questions and answer choices with students. If students are having difficulty, provide them with additional practice items.

UNIT 3 Spelling

Lesson 3: Identifying Word Spellings

Directions: Darken the circle for the word that is <u>not</u> spelled correctly. Darken the circle for *No mistakes* if all the words are spelled correctly.

> **TRY THIS**
> First, decide which words you know are spelled correctly. Then, look at the remaining words to make your choice. Be sure to look at all the words.

S1 A adjust
    B climate
    C dele
    D earn
    E *(No mistakes)*

 THINK IT THROUGH The correct answer is <u>C</u>. The word dele is spelled incorrectly. The correct spelling is d-e-a-l. The other choices are spelled correctly.

STOP

1 A shufful
   B seek
   C mess
   D rely
   E *(No mistakes)*

2 J hotel
   K seal
   L remind
   M gitar
   N *(No mistakes)*

3 A thrill
   B cliff
   C indeed
   D jacket
   E *(No mistakes)*

4 J bakteria
   K dandelion
   L unexpected
   M beckon
   N *(No mistakes)*

5 A spectacle
   B celery
   C quantity
   D walz
   E *(No mistakes)*

6 J sensible
   K fordge
   L remedy
   M mansion
   N *(No mistakes)*

7 A instruction
   B distinguish
   C nesessity
   D triangle
   E *(No mistakes)*

8 J laundry
   K abanden
   L transfer
   M success
   N *(No mistakes)*

9 A irregular
   B satisfactory
   C organiz
   D radar
   E *(No mistakes)*

GO ON

Level 12

Answers
S1 Ⓐ Ⓑ ● Ⓓ Ⓔ   2 Ⓙ Ⓚ Ⓛ ● Ⓝ   4 ● Ⓚ Ⓛ Ⓜ Ⓝ   6 Ⓙ ● Ⓛ Ⓜ Ⓝ   8 Ⓙ ● Ⓛ Ⓜ Ⓝ
1 ● Ⓑ Ⓒ Ⓓ Ⓔ   3 Ⓐ Ⓑ Ⓒ Ⓓ ●   5 Ⓐ Ⓑ Ⓒ ● Ⓔ   7 Ⓐ Ⓑ ● Ⓓ Ⓔ   9 Ⓐ Ⓑ ● Ⓓ Ⓔ

13

UNIT 3 Spelling

Lesson 3: Identifying Word Spellings

Language Skill: Identifying correct spellings of words

SAY: **Turn to Lesson 3, Identifying Word Spellings, on page 13.**

Check to see that all students find Lesson 3.

SAY: **In Lesson 3 you will practice finding correct spellings of words.**

Read the <u>Directions</u> to students.

SAY: **Now look at Try This.**

Read <u>Try This</u> to students.

SAY: **Now look at S1. Read the answer choices carefully. Then darken the circle for the word that is not spelled correctly. Darken the circle for *No mistakes* if all the words are spelled correctly.**

Allow students time to find and mark their answer.

SAY: **Now look at Think It Through.**

Read <u>Think It Through</u> to students. Check to see that all students have filled in the correct answer space. Ask students if they have any questions.

SAY: **Now you will practice finding the correct spellings for more words. Do numbers 1 through 27 just as we did S1. When you come to the words *GO ON* at the bottom of page 13, continue working on the next page. When you come to the word *STOP* at the bottom of page 14, put your pencils down. You may now begin.**

Allow students time to find and mark their answers.

10	J league	16	J ingury	22	J disappear
	K vertical		K impressive		K develop
	L academy		L neon		L despair
	M desend		M lecturer		M desireable
	N *(No mistakes)*		N *(No mistakes)*		N *(No mistakes)*

11	A height	17	A happened	23	A solution
	B raspberries		B technical		B bureau
	C theary		C rath		C urban
	D tornado		D disobey		D vanilla
	E *(No mistakes)*		E *(No mistakes)*		E *(No mistakes)*

12	J dense	18	J kneed	24	J panel
	K liquide		K elevate		K recover
	L pamphlet		L ornament		L restrant
	M fascinate		M tense		M garlic
	N *(No mistakes)*		N *(No mistakes)*		N *(No mistakes)*

13	A isicle	19	A nitrogen	25	A artic
	B dazzle		B baffel		B impolite
	C tremendous		C stingy		C blemish
	D wavelength		D peddle		D whisk
	E *(No mistakes)*		E *(No mistakes)*		E *(No mistakes)*

14	J throughout	20	J imply	26	J compleetly
	K benefit		K opertunity		K carbon
	L yolk		L patron		L fortify
	M disbeleif		M binder		M semester
	N *(No mistakes)*		N *(No mistakes)*		N *(No mistakes)*

15	A gauge	21	A forty	27	A majority
	B illustrate		B gigantic		B relation
	C seige		C flatter		C crease
	D sanitary		D bizniss		D torpedo
	E *(No mistakes)*		E *(No mistakes)*		E *(No mistakes)*

STOP

Answers

10 J K L ● N   14 J K L ● N   18 ● K L M N   22 J K L ● N   26 ● K L M N

11 A B ● D E   15 A B ● D E   19 A ● C D E   23 A B C D ●   27 A B C D ●

12 J ● L M N   16 ● K L M N   20 J ● L M N   24 J K ● M N

13 ● B C D E   17 A B ● D E   21 A B C ● E   25 ● B C D E

Level 12

14

Unit 3 Test

S1
- A tissue
- B nazal
- C weird
- D cartridge
- E *(No mistakes)*

STOP

For questions 1–16, darken the circle for the word that is **not** spelled correctly. Darken the circle for *No mistakes* if all the words are spelled correctly.

1
- A rummage
- B vacant
- C agreement
- D decreace
- E *(No mistakes)*

2
- J medical
- K burnt
- L prinsipal
- M wheelchair
- N *(No mistakes)*

3
- A cazully
- B pain
- C tusk
- D foster
- E *(No mistakes)*

4
- J gasoline
- K label
- L actres
- M author
- N (No mistakes)

5
- A investagate
- B antenna
- C depth
- D dismal
- E *(No mistakes)*

6
- J defrost
- K forfit
- L compact
- M positive
- N *(No mistakes)*

7
- A clothes
- B telegram
- C introduce
- D gust
- E *(No mistakes)*

8
- J crumpeld
- K utensil
- L translate
- M junction
- N *(No mistakes)*

9
- A majestic
- B alegiance
- C elastic
- D porcelain
- E *(No mistakes)*

10
- J candidate
- K absence
- L conservation
- M register
- N *(No mistakes)*

11
- A attendance
- B citizenship
- C antique
- D deth
- E *(No mistakes)*

12
- J geography
- K sandwich
- L vulture
- M schedyule
- N *(No mistakes)*

13
- A accidently
- B authority
- C accept
- D autograph
- E *(No mistakes)*

14
- J shingles
- K increse
- L marriage
- M elevation
- N *(No mistakes)*

15
- A dissolve
- B displease
- C dispute
- D dispose
- E *(No mistakes)*

16
- J item
- K momentary
- L indent
- M texture
- N (No mistakes)

STOP

Answers

S1 Ⓐ ● Ⓒ Ⓓ Ⓔ   4 Ⓙ Ⓚ ● Ⓜ Ⓝ   8 ● Ⓚ Ⓛ Ⓜ Ⓝ   12 Ⓙ Ⓚ Ⓛ ● Ⓝ   16 Ⓙ Ⓚ Ⓛ Ⓜ ●
1 Ⓐ Ⓑ Ⓒ ● Ⓔ   5 ● Ⓑ Ⓒ Ⓓ Ⓔ   9 Ⓐ ● Ⓒ Ⓓ Ⓔ   13 ● Ⓑ Ⓒ Ⓓ Ⓔ
2 Ⓙ Ⓚ ● Ⓜ Ⓝ   6 Ⓙ ● Ⓛ Ⓜ Ⓝ   10 Ⓙ Ⓚ Ⓛ Ⓜ ●   14 Ⓙ ● Ⓛ Ⓜ Ⓝ
3 ● Ⓑ Ⓒ Ⓓ Ⓔ   7 Ⓐ Ⓑ Ⓒ Ⓓ ●   11 Ⓐ Ⓑ Ⓒ ● Ⓔ   15 Ⓐ Ⓑ Ⓒ Ⓓ ●

Level 12

15

Unit 3 Test

SAY: **Turn to the Unit 3 Test on page 15.**

Check to see that all students find the Unit 3 Test.

SAY: **In this test you will use the language skills that we have practiced in this unit. Look at S1. We will work the sample exercise together before you begin the test. Read the answer choices carefully. Then darken the circle for the word that is not spelled correctly. Darken the circle for *No mistakes* if all the words are spelled correctly.**

Allow students time to find and mark their answer.

SAY: **You should have darkened the circle for *B* because it shows an incorrect spelling for the word *nasal*.**

Check to see that all students have filled in the correct answer space. Ask students if they have any questions.

SAY: **Now you will finish the test on your own. Read the directions carefully. Do numbers 1 through 16 just as we did the sample. Read the answer choices carefully. Then darken the circle for each correct answer. When you come to the word *STOP* at the bottom of page 15, put your pencils down. You may now begin.**

Allow students time to find and mark their answers.

SAY: **It is now time to stop. You have completed the Unit 3 Test. Make sure that you have carefully filled in your answer spaces and have completely erased any stray marks. Then put your pencils down.**

After the test has been scored, review the questions and answer choices with students. If students are having difficulty with any lesson, provide them with additional practice items.

UNIT 4 Language Mechanics

Lesson 4: Using Correct Capitalization

Directions: Darken the circle for the line that has a capitalization error. Darken the circle for *No mistakes* if there is no capitalization error.

> **TRY THIS**
> Study each line to find a word that should be capitalized or a word that should not be capitalized. Remember that proper nouns are capitalized, but common nouns are not capitalized.

S1 A My grandmother has lived in
    B her home on Pontiac Avenue
    C for almost 45 years.
    D *(No mistakes)*

> **THINK IT THROUGH**
> The correct answer is D. There are no capitalization errors in this sentence. Do not capitalize grandmother because it is a common noun. Capitalize Pontiac Avenue because it is a proper noun.

STOP

1 A We have italian food for
   B dinner on Sunday nights. It
   C is a special treat that I love!
   D *(No mistakes)*

2 J Rosie asked her sister,
   K "Do you want to go swimming
   L after school on Friday?"
   M *(No mistakes)*

3 A When my mom was younger,
   B she watched only three hours
   C of Television each week.
   D *(No mistakes)*

4 J Most children go back to school
   K just before labor day
   L in early September.
   M *(No mistakes)*

5 A   3 Beach Street
   B   narragansett, RI 02882
   C   July 29, 1995
   D *(No mistakes)*

6 J dear Grandma,
   K I'd like to invite you to spend next
   L weekend at our house.
   M *(No mistakes)*

7 A Mom, Dad, and i plan to take you
   B to a movie. Then we will eat at
   C your favorite restaurant, The Pier.
   D *(No mistakes)*

8 J Please say you will come!
   K   your grandson,
   L   *Eddie*
   M *(No mistakes)*

STOP
Level 12

Answers
S1 Ⓐ Ⓑ Ⓒ ●
1 ● Ⓑ Ⓒ Ⓓ
2 Ⓙ Ⓚ Ⓛ ●
3 Ⓐ Ⓑ ● Ⓓ
4 Ⓙ ● Ⓛ Ⓜ
5 Ⓐ ● Ⓒ Ⓓ
6 ● Ⓚ Ⓛ Ⓜ
7 ● Ⓑ Ⓒ Ⓓ
8 Ⓙ ● Ⓛ Ⓜ

16

UNIT 4 Language Mechanics

Lesson 4: Using Correct Capitalization

Language Skill: Recognizing errors in capitalization; identifying correct capitalization in sentences

SAY: **Turn to Lesson 4, Using Correct Capitalization, on page 16.**

Check to see that all students find Lesson 4.

SAY: **In Lesson 4 you will practice finding errors in capitalization as well as practice identifying correct capitalization for sentences.**

Read the Directions to students.

SAY: **Now look at Try This.**

Read Try This to students.

SAY: **Now look at S1. Read the sentence. Then darken the circle for the line that shows a capitalization error. Darken the circle for *No mistakes* if there is no capitalization error.**

Allow students time to find and mark their answer.

SAY: **Now look at Think It Through.**

Read Think It Through to students. Check to see that all students have filled in the correct answer space. Ask students if they have any questions.

SAY: **Now you will practice finding errors in capitalization and practice identifying correct capitalization for more sentences. Do numbers 1 through 8 just as we did S1. When you come to the word *STOP* at the bottom of page 16, put your pencils down. You may now begin.**

Allow students time to find and mark their answers.

Review the questions and answer choices with students. Discuss with the class why one answer is correct and the others are not correct. Also check to see that students have carefully filled in the answer spaces and have completely erased any stray marks.

Lesson 5: Using Correct Punctuation

Directions: Darken the circle for the line that has a punctuation error. Darken the circle for *No mistakes* if there is no punctuation error.

TRY THIS

Read the sentence carefully. Think about where you would put the punctuation marks if you were writing the sentence. Look carefully for punctuation marks that are missing, that are in the wrong place, or that should not be there at all.

S1
A Do you know why a grasshopper can
B jump so high A grasshopper has
C powerful muscles in its back legs.
D *(No mistakes)*

THINK IT THROUGH

The correct answer is B. All sentences end with a punctuation mark. A question mark should end the sentence "Do you know why a grasshopper can jump so high?"

STOP

1
A We always hope it wont rain
B on the Fourth of July because we
C look forward to seeing the fireworks.
D *(No mistakes)*

2
J On the museum tour, Ms. Clare
K told us, "The blue, whale is the
L largest animal on Earth today."
M *(No mistakes)*

3
A My father a writer for the newspaper
B won an award for his article on
C school recycling programs.
D *(No mistakes)*

4
J Hans Christian Anderson wrote many
K fairy tales. The Nightingale is
L one of my favorite stories.
M *(No mistakes)*

5
A   212 Byrnes Dr.
B   McLean Virginia 22101
C   August 28, 1995
D *(No mistakes)*

6
J Charts Moving Company
K Cranston, Rhode Island   02910
L Dear Mr. Gordon:
M *(No mistakes)*

7
A When we moved, we hired your
B company. Your movers were
C friendly and did a good job.
D *(No mistakes)*

8
J We were pleased with the service.
K   Sincerely yours.
L
M *(No mistakes)*

STOP

Level 12

Answers
S1 Ⓐ ● Ⓒ Ⓓ   2 Ⓙ ● Ⓛ Ⓜ   4 Ⓙ ● Ⓛ Ⓜ   6 Ⓙ Ⓚ Ⓛ ●   8 Ⓙ ● Ⓛ Ⓜ
1 ● Ⓑ Ⓒ Ⓓ   3 ● Ⓑ Ⓒ Ⓓ   5 Ⓐ ● Ⓒ Ⓓ   7 Ⓐ Ⓑ Ⓒ ●

17

Lesson 5: Using Correct Punctuation

Language Skill: Recognizing errors in punctuation; identifying correct punctuation in sentences

SAY: **Turn to Lesson 5, Using Correct Punctuation, on page 17.**

Check to see that all students find Lesson 5.

SAY: **In Lesson 5 you will practice finding errors in punctuation as well as practice identifying correct punctuation for sentences.**

Read the Directions to students.

SAY: **Now look at Try This.**

Read Try This to students.

SAY: **Now look at S1. Read the sentences. Then darken the circle for the line that has a punctuation error. Darken the circle for *No mistakes* if there is no punctuation error.**

Allow students time to find and mark their answer.

SAY: **Now look at Think It Through.**

Read Think It Through to students. Check to see that all students have filled in the correct answer space. Ask students if they have any questions.

SAY: **Now you will practice finding errors in punctuation and practice identifying correct punctuation for more sentences. Do numbers 1 through 8 just as we did S1. When you come to the word *STOP* at the bottom of page 17, put your pencils down. You may now begin.**

Allow students time to find and mark their answers.

Review the questions and answer choices with students. Discuss with the class why one answer is correct and the others are not correct. Also check to see that students have carefully filled in the answer spaces and have completely erased any stray marks.

Unit 4 Test

S1
A All of the grandchildren give
B Aunt Teresa a kiss every
C time they see her.
D *(No mistakes)*

STOP

S2
J My brother, and I bring lots
K of travel games to play in
L the car when we go on a trip.
M *(No mistakes)*

STOP

For questions 1–11, darken the circle for the line that has a capitalization error. Darken the circle for *No mistakes* if there is no capitalization error.

1
A People travel from all over the world
B to see the statue of Liberty. It was
C given to the United States by France.
D *(No mistakes)*

2
J Julia's Grandfather owns a
K Swedish bakery. It is
L located on Langer Avenue.
M *(No mistakes)*

3
A my Uncle Mac always takes
B his lunch to work with
C him on Friday mornings.
D *(No mistakes)*

4
J For the school show last year,
K I wrote a scary poem called
L "Watch out for the goblins."
M *(No mistakes)*

5
A My mother and I went to the
B Palmer Museum to see the
C new Dinosaur exhibit.
D *(No mistakes)*

6
J E. B. White, the author of
K *Charlotte's web*, wrote
L other children's books as well.
M *(No mistakes)*

7
A Our teacher, Ms. Webster, showed
B us slides from her european trip.
C I liked the ones of France the best.
D *(No mistakes)*

8
J The National Audubon Society
K works to save places where birds
L live. It teaches people about birds.
M *(No mistakes)*

9
A The Public Library is one of
B my favorite places in town.
C I go there every Saturday.
D *(No mistakes)*

10
J The planet Mercury is closer
K to the sun than any other
L planet, including Earth.
M *(No mistakes)*

11
A In March, I got a very special
B surprise for my birthday—a
C german shepherd puppy!
D *(No mistakes)*

GO ON

Answers

S1 Ⓐ Ⓑ Ⓒ ●
S2 ● Ⓚ Ⓛ Ⓜ

18
1 Ⓐ ● Ⓒ Ⓓ
2 ● Ⓚ Ⓛ Ⓜ
3 ● Ⓑ Ⓒ Ⓓ
4 Ⓙ Ⓚ ● Ⓜ

5 Ⓐ Ⓑ ● Ⓓ
6 Ⓙ ● Ⓛ Ⓜ
7 Ⓐ ● Ⓒ Ⓓ

8 Ⓙ Ⓚ ● Ⓜ
9 ● Ⓑ Ⓒ Ⓓ
10 Ⓙ Ⓚ Ⓛ ●

11 Ⓐ Ⓑ ● Ⓓ

Level 12

Unit 4 Test

SAY: **Turn to the Unit 4 Test on page 18.**

Check to see that all students find the Unit 4 Test.

SAY: **In this test you will use the language skills that we have practiced in this unit. We will work the samples together before you begin the test. Look at S1. Read the sentence. Then darken the circle for the line that has a capitalization error. Darken the circle for *No mistakes* if there is no capitalization error.**

Allow students time to find and mark their answer.

SAY: **You should have darkened the circle for *D* because there is no capitalization error.**

Check to see that all students have filled in the correct answer space. Ask students if they have any questions.

SAY: **Now look at S2. Read the sentence. Then darken the circle for the line that shows a punctuation error. Darken the circle for *No mistakes* if there is no punctuation error.**

Allow students time to find and mark their answers.

SAY: **You should have darkened the circle for *J* because it has a punctuation error. A comma is not needed in the line.**

Check to see that all students have filled in the correct answer space. Ask students if they have any questions.

SAY: **Now you will finish the test on your own. Read the directions for each section carefully. Do numbers 1 through 24 just as we did the samples. Read the sentences carefully. Then darken the circle for each correct answer. When you come to the words *GO ON* at the bottom of page 18, continue working on the next page. When you come to the word *STOP* at the bottom of page 19, put your pencils down. You may now begin.**

Allow students time to find and mark their answers.

After the test has been scored, review the questions and answer choices with students. If students are having difficulty, provide them with additional practice items.

For questions 12–24, darken the circle for the line that has a punctuation error. Darken the circle for *No mistakes* if there is no punctuation error.

12 J Because Tucson Arizona has
   K such a hot climate, many people
   L own swimming pools.
   M *(No Mistakes)*

13 A Robert does not like most
   B flavors of yogurt, except for
   C lemon strawberry and, vanilla.
   D *(No mistakes)*

14 J Susi's favorite game is Monopoly.
   K She likes to be the banker and
   L always asks "me to play with her."
   M *(No mistakes)*

15 A Mr. García who leads the pet parade
   B is moving to another city. Would
   C you like to take his place next year?
   D *(No mistakes)*

16 J On Sunday my little cousin and
   K I spent the day together. She asked
   L me a thousand times "What's that?"
   M *(No mistakes)*

17 A Lee has a new pair of tennis shoe's.
   B He plans to wear them during
   C the March of Dimes walkathon.
   D *(No mistakes)*

18 J Miss Noguchi Jane's terrific
   K first-grade teacher, used to
   L teach third grade at my school.
   M *(No mistakes)*

19 A There are many names for the
   B game of table tennis The most
   C common name is Ping-Pong.
   D *(No mistakes)*

20 J The hotel in Mississippi where
   K we stayed last summer,
   L was built after the Civil War.
   M *(No mistakes)*

21 A   68 Westfield Drive
   B   Quincy, MA 01258
   C   January 2 1995
   D *(No mistakes)*

22 J Twin Oaks Restaurant
   K Newport, MA 01243
   L Dear Management.
   M *(No mistakes)*

23 A My family visited your restaurant
   B last night. Even my fussy brother
   C exclaimed, "I love this food!"
   D *(No mistakes)*

24 J Well come again soon!
   K   Yours truly,
   L
   M *(No mistakes)*

STOP

Answers
12 ● Ⓚ Ⓛ Ⓜ   15 ● Ⓑ Ⓒ Ⓓ   18 ● Ⓚ Ⓛ Ⓜ   21 Ⓐ Ⓑ ● Ⓓ   24 ● Ⓚ Ⓛ Ⓜ   Level 12
13 Ⓐ Ⓑ ● Ⓓ   16 Ⓙ Ⓚ ● Ⓜ   19 Ⓐ ● Ⓒ Ⓓ   22 Ⓙ Ⓚ ● Ⓜ
14 Ⓙ Ⓚ ● Ⓜ   17 ● Ⓑ Ⓒ Ⓓ   20 Ⓙ ● Ⓛ Ⓜ   23 Ⓐ Ⓑ Ⓒ ●   **19**

UNIT 5 Language Expression

Lesson 6: Determining Usage

Directions: Darken the circle for the line that has an error in the way the words are used. Darken the circle for *No mistakes* if all the words are used correctly.

TRY THIS
Look at each line carefully. When you read the sentences, listen for the word or phrase that sounds incorrect.

S1
A "I wish I could just lay down,"
B said my mom. "I'm exhausted
C from all the driving we did!"
D (No mistakes)

THINK IT THROUGH
The correct answer is A. The verb lay is used incorrectly. Lay means to put something down. The correct verb is lie. Lie means to rest or to be in a reclining position.

STOP

1
A The teacher wondered to
B who Ray was speaking when
C he yelled, "Do it yourself!"
D (No mistakes)

2
J Haven't you never been to
K Lisa Biro's house? She lives
L right around the corner from you.
M (No mistakes)

3
A My favoritest actor is Sam
B Neill. He was really good in
C the movie *Jurassic Park*.
D (No mistakes)

4
J It is so much fun to watch the
K kitten try to wash hisself. He
L just rolls all over the floor.
M (No mistakes)

5
A The choir concert was very
B entertaining. We were all
C amazed at how well Stacy singed.
D (No mistakes)

6
J My father and me cooked pizza
K last night, and everyone, even
L my sister, said it was delicious.
M (No mistakes)

7
A My best friend wants to know
B how to play the game Scrabble,
C so I'm learning her how to play it.
D (No mistakes)

8
J I should ought to have done
K my chores earlier. Now I'm too
L tired even to think about them!
M (No mistakes)

9
A My brother and sister go to the
B library every week. They always
C check out too many books.
D (No mistakes)

10
J When we got to the mall, Dad
K said, "Let's all meet back here
L at the fountain in three hours."
M (No mistakes)

STOP

Answers
S1 ● Ⓑ Ⓒ Ⓓ
1 Ⓐ ● Ⓒ Ⓓ
2 ● Ⓚ Ⓛ Ⓜ
3 ● Ⓑ Ⓒ Ⓓ
4 Ⓙ ● Ⓛ Ⓜ
5 Ⓐ Ⓑ ● Ⓓ
6 ● Ⓚ Ⓛ Ⓜ
7 Ⓐ Ⓑ ● Ⓓ
8 ● Ⓚ Ⓛ Ⓜ
9 Ⓐ Ⓑ Ⓒ ●
10 Ⓙ Ⓚ Ⓛ ●

Level 12

20

UNIT 5 Language Expression

Lesson 6: Determining Usage

Language Skills: Determining the appropriate use of verbs, pronouns, adjectives, and adverbs in sentences

SAY: **Turn to Lesson 6, Determining Usage, on page 20.**

Check to see that all students find Lesson 6.

SAY: **In Lesson 6 you will practice identifying the incorrect usage and recognizing correct usage of words within sentences.**

Read the <u>Directions</u> to students.

SAY: **Now look at <u>Try This</u>.**

Read <u>Try This</u> to students.

SAY: **Now look at S1. Read the sentences carefully. Then darken the circle for the line that has an error in the way words are used. Darken the circle for *No mistakes* if all the words are used correctly.**

Allow students time to find and mark their answer.

SAY: **Now look at <u>Think It Through</u>.**

Read <u>Think It Through</u> to students. Check to see that all students have filled in the correct answer space. Ask students if they have any questions.

SAY: **Now you will practice identifying the incorrect usage and recognizing correct usage of words in more sentences. Do numbers 1 through 10 just as we did S1. When you come to the word *STOP* at the bottom of page 20, put your pencils down. You may now begin.**

Allow students time to find and mark their answers.

Review the questions and answer choices with students. Discuss with the class why one answer is correct and the others are not correct. Also check to see that students have carefully filled in the answer spaces and have completely erased any stray marks.

Lesson 7: Analyzing Paragraphs

Directions: Darken the circle for the correct answer to each question. Darken the circle for *No change* if the sentence is correct as it is.

> **TRY THIS**
> After you have read the paragraph carefully, read each question and each answer choice before you choose your answer. Refer to the paragraph to check your answers.

S1

¹ Hopi Indians lived in the southwest part of the United States, in an area we now call Arizona. ² They have been making most of what they needed to live. ³ They made pottery for their dishes and grew cotton which they used to make clothing. ⁴ They were always growing their own food. ⁵ Farming was difficult, however, because the land was dry. ⁶ Today Arizona is known for its hot desert climate. ⁷ Since the Hopis were religious people, they prayed for the rain they needed.

Which sentence does **not** belong in this paragraph?

A Sentence 2   C Sentence 5

B Sentence 4   D Sentence 6

THINK IT THROUGH The correct answer is D. The topic of this paragraph is the Hopi Indians. Sentence 6 describes Arizona's climate, not the Hopi Indians. Sentence 6 does not belong in this paragraph.

STOP

Use the paragraph in S1 to answer questions 1–4.

1 **What is the best opening sentence to add to this paragraph?**

A When I went to Arizona, I visited the Hopi reservation.

B Many Hopi Indians still live in the southwest today.

C I have learned a lot about Native Americans in my social studies class.

D In ancient times, many Native American tribes lived in various regions of North America.

2 **What is the best way to write the underlined part of sentence 4?**

J grew their own food

K had always planned to grow all their own food

L were always eating food they grew themselves

M *(No change)*

3 **Choose the best way to write the underlined part of sentence 2.**

A were making

B made

C always did make

D *(No change)*

4 **What is the best concluding sentence to add to this paragraph?**

J The Hopis believed that the kachinas would always protect them.

K The Hopi Indians have always been a proud and independent people.

L The Hopi Indians preferred to live in a wet climate.

M Those living on the Hopi reservation today still try to farm the dry land and make money from selling pottery, jewelry, and baskets.

STOP

Answers
S1 Ⓐ Ⓑ Ⓒ ●   2 ● Ⓚ Ⓛ Ⓜ   4 Ⓙ Ⓚ Ⓛ ●
1 Ⓐ Ⓑ Ⓒ ●   3 Ⓐ ● Ⓒ Ⓓ

Lesson 7: Analyzing Paragraphs

Language Skills: Determining the topic and supporting details of a paragraph; identifying information that does not belong in a paragraph; determining word usage in the context of a paragraph

SAY: **Turn to Lesson 7, Analyzing Paragraphs, on page 21.**

Check to see that all students find Lesson 7.

SAY: **In Lesson 7 you will practice analyzing paragraphs.**

Read the Directions to students.

SAY: **Now look at Try This.**

Read Try This to students.

SAY: **Now look at S1. Read the paragraph silently. Then read the question and answer choices carefully. Darken the circle for the choice that shows the sentence that does not belong in the paragraph.**

Allow students time to find and mark their answer.

SAY: **Now look at Think It Through.**

Read Think It Through to students. Check to see that all students have filled in the correct answer space. Ask students if they have any questions.

SAY: **Now you will practice further analyzing the paragraph. Do numbers 1 through 4 just as we did S1. When you come to the word *STOP* at the bottom of page 21, put your pencils down. You may now begin.**

Allow students time to find and mark their answers.

Review the questions and answer choices with students. Discuss with the class why one answer is correct and the others are not correct. Also check to see that students have carefully filled in the answer spaces and have completely erased any stray marks.

Lesson 8: Expressing Ideas Clearly

Directions: Darken the circle for the sentence or sentences that express the idea most clearly.

TRY THIS | Read each answer choice carefully. Look for the sentence or sentences that are well organized, complete, and contain no unclear references.

S1 A On our vacation we will be climbing mountains and to ride bicycles.
    B On our vacation we will be climbing mountains and riding bicycles.
    C On our vacation we will climb mountains and riding bicycles.
    D Our vacation will have mountains to climb and riding bicycles.

THINK IT THROUGH | The correct answer is B because it clearly expresses the idea. It is a complete, correct sentence whose verbs have the same form.

STOP

1 A In the afternoon exactly I get out of school at 2:45 P.M.
   B At 2:45 P.M. I get out of school. This is exactly every day.
   C Every day in the afternoon I get exactly out of school at 2:45 P.M.
   D Every day, I get out of school at exactly 2:45 P.M.

2 J The boys fought and argued over who would use the new computer.
   K The boys fought over using the new computer and argued about it, too.
   L The boys argued and fought. Who would use the new computer?
   M The boys argued about who would use the new computer they just got new.

3 A Lucia showed off her new bracelet on her arm which was gold.
   B Being gold, Lucia showed off her new bracelet on her arm.
   C Lucia showed off the new gold bracelet that was on her arm.
   D Lucia showed off, on her arm, the new bracelet, being gold.

4 J Frank received a new racing bike as a birthday present.
   K As a present, Frank received on his birthday a new racing bike.
   L Receiving a new racing bike, Frank got a birthday present.
   M Frank, as a birthday present. He received a new racing bike.

GO ON

Level 12

Answers
S1 (A) ● (C) (D)   2 ● (K) (L) (M)   4 ● (K) (L) (M)
22
1 (A) (B) (C) ●   3 (A) (B) ● (D)

Lesson 8: Expressing Ideas Clearly

Language Skill: Identifying sentences that are the clearest, most concise, and best examples of effective writing

SAY: **Turn to Lesson 8, Expressing Ideas Clearly, on page 22.**

Check to see that all students find Lesson 8.

SAY: **In Lesson 8 you will practice identifying the sentence or sentences that express the idea most clearly.**

Read the Directions to students.

SAY: **Now look at Try This.**

Read Try This to students.

SAY: **Now look at S1. Read the sentences silently. Then darken the circle for the choice that shows the sentence or sentences that express the idea most clearly.**

Allow students time to find and mark their answer.

SAY: **Now look at Think It Through.**

Read Think It Through to students. Check to see that all students have filled in the correct answer space. Ask students if they have any questions.

SAY: **Now you will practice identifying more sentences that express an idea most clearly. Do numbers 1 through 8 just as we did S1. Read the question to number 9 carefully. Then choose the correct answer. When you come to the words *GO ON* at the bottom of page 22, continue working on the next page. When you come to the word *STOP* at the bottom of page 23, put your pencils down. You may now begin.**

Allow students time to find and mark their answers.

5　A　Our poodle blocked Ed's view while watching television.

　　B　Our poodle, while watching television, blocked Ed's view.

　　C　While Ed was watching television, our poodle blocked his view.

　　D　While watching television, our poodle blocked Ed's view.

6　J　He can't feel it now, but Jerome's neck hurt this morning.

　　K　The neck which hurt Jerome this morning went away.

　　L　Jerome can't feel his neck which hurt him this morning.

　　M　Jerome's neck hurt this morning, but the pain has gone away.

7　A　When Belinda saw the sky, she wanted to be in a plane in it.

　　B　Belinda saw a plane in the sky, and she wanted to be in it.

　　C　Seeing the sky and the plane, Belinda wanted to be in it.

　　D　Belinda wanted to be in the sky and the plane she saw.

8　J　The children performing on stage they did not appear nervous.

　　K　The children performing on stage did not appear nervous.

　　L　The children on stage. Did not appear nervous performing.

　　M　The children performing. On stage they did not appear nervous.

9　Which would be most appropriate for requesting a camp catalog and application form?

A　Please send me your camp catalog along with an application form as soon as possible. I hope to go to your camp this summer!

C　If you don't send me your camp catalog and application form immediately, I will go to another camp this summer. My name and address are on the back of the envelope.

B　A few of my friends have been to your camp. They like it, but they say the food isn't that good. I'd like you to send me a catalog and application form in case I decide to go there.

D　Rush me a copy of your camp catalog and an application. I really want to go to your camp, but if your application form comes too late, I won't be able to. That will be your fault.

STOP

Answers

5 Ⓐ Ⓑ ● Ⓓ　　7 Ⓐ ● Ⓒ Ⓓ　　9 ● Ⓑ Ⓒ Ⓓ

6 Ⓙ Ⓚ Ⓛ ●　　8 Ⓙ ● Ⓛ Ⓜ

Directions: Darken the circle for the word or words that best fit in the underlined part of the sentence. Darken the circle for *No change* if the sentence is correct as it is.

> **TRY THIS**
> Ask yourself whether the underlined word or words make sense in the sentence. Then reread the sentence using each answer choice in place of the underlined part of the sentence.

S1 When we see each other in July, school **was** over.

A had been

B is being

C will be

D *(No change)*

> **THINK IT THROUGH**
> The sentence is about something that will happen in the future. Therefore, the underlined verb must be in the future tense. The correct answer is C.

STOP

---

1 It's easier for me to do my homework **until** it is quiet.

A when

B so that

C unless

D *(No change)*

2 Now that it is springtime, we **did get** plenty of rainy weather.

J will be getting

K had been getting

L got

M *(No change)*

3 **Except** you fall asleep while taking it, you'll do well on the test.

A Unless

B Besides

C Since

D *(No change)*

4 No matter how well the Jets play, I'll be their fan **that** I live in New York.

J but

K as long as

L during

M *(No change)*

5 Michael enjoys his hobby, **building and painting** model airplanes.

A building, painting

B to build and to paint

C being the building and painting of

D *(No change)*

6 We are always reminded to brush and floss our teeth **until** bedtime.

J while

K before

L since

M *(No change)*

STOP

Level 12

Answers

S1 Ⓐ Ⓑ ● Ⓓ   **2** ● Ⓚ Ⓛ Ⓜ   **4** Ⓙ ● Ⓛ Ⓜ   **6** Ⓙ ● Ⓛ Ⓜ

1 ● Ⓑ Ⓒ Ⓓ   **3** ● Ⓑ Ⓒ Ⓓ   **5** Ⓐ Ⓑ Ⓒ ●

24

Lesson 9: Choosing Correct Words and Phrases

Language Skill: Identifying the words and phrases that best fit in the context of a sentence

SAY: **Turn to Lesson 9, Choosing Correct Words and Phrases, on page 24.**

Check to see that all students find Lesson 9.

SAY: **In Lesson 9 you will practice identifying the words or words that best fit in a sentence.**

Read the Directions to students.

SAY: **Now look at Try This.**

Read Try This to students.

SAY: **Now look at S1. Read the sentence silently. Then darken the circle for the word or words that best fit in the sentence. Darken the circle for *No change* if the sentence is correct as it is.**

Allow students time to find and mark their answer.

SAY: **Now look at Think It Through.**

Read Think It Through to students. Check to see that all students have filled in the correct answer space. Ask students if they have any questions.

SAY: **Now you will practice identifying more words that best fit in a sentence. Do numbers 1 through 6 just as we did S1. When you come to the word *STOP* at the bottom of page 24, put your pencils down. You may now begin.**

Allow students time to find and mark their answers.

Review the questions and answer choices with students. Discuss with the class why one answer is correct and the others are not correct. Also check to see that students have carefully filled in the answer spaces and have completely erased any stray marks.

Unit 5 Test

S1
- A To me, sunny days are more better
- B than rainy days because there are
- C so many things to do outside.
- D *(No mistakes)*

STOP

For questions 1–5, darken the circle for the line that has an error in the way the words are used. Darken the circle for *No mistakes* if all the words are used correctly.

1
- A Our teacher expects us to
- B rays our hands if we have
- C something to say in class.
- D *(No mistakes)*

2
- J "Where did you put them peanuts
- K that I brought home last night?"
- L Simeon's mother asked him.
- M *(No mistakes)*

3
- A Mary knowed how to keep
- B secrets. She never tells anyone
- C about the things we talk about.
- D *(No mistakes)*

4
- J Just because we don't like her
- K brother doesn't mean we
- L shouldn't go to her party.
- M *(No mistakes)*

5
- A One of my friends brought
- B their camera to the beach
- C and took many pictures of us.
- D *(No mistakes)*

For questions 6–9, read the paragraph. Then darken the circle for each correct answer.

> [1] My sister and I like to stay overnight at our grandparents' house. [2] Grandma and Granddad take us to the movies and out to dinner. [3] At home, we hardly ever do anything exciting. [4] But the best part is bedtime so that Granddad always tells us one of his spooky stories. [5] When we go out to dinner, we can order whatever we want.

6 Which sentence does not belong in this paragraph?
- J Sentence 1
- K Sentence 2
- L Sentence 3
- M Sentence 5

7 Choose the best opening sentence for this paragraph.
- A My parents let me spend every weekend at my grandparents' house.
- B Sleeping at a friend's house overnight is great.
- C We always have fun when we're with our grandparents.
- D Do you ever have sleep-overs?

8 What is the best way to write the underlined part of sentence 4?
- J because Granddad
- K so that he
- L unless Granddad
- M during Granddad

9 What is the best place for sentence 5 in the paragraph?
- A Where it is now
- B Between sentences 1 and 2
- C Between sentences 3 and 4
- D After sentence 2

GO ON

Level 12

Answers

S1 ● B C D	2 ● K L M	4 J K L ●	6 J K ● M	8 ● K L M
1 A ● C D	3 ● B C D	5 A ● C D	7 A B ● D	9 A B C ●

25

Unit 5 Test

SAY: **Turn to the Unit 5 Test on page 25.**

Check to see that all students find the Unit 5 Test.

SAY: **In this test you will use the language skills that we have practiced in this unit. This test is divided into five parts. We will work the sample together before you begin the test. Look at S1. Read the answer choices carefully. Then darken the circle for the line that has an error in the way words are used. Darken the circle for *No mistakes* if all the words are used correctly.**

Allow students time to find and mark their answer.

SAY: **You should have darkened the circle for *A* because the words *more better* show incorrect usage.**

Check to see that all students have filled in the correct answer space. Ask students if they have any questions.

SAY: **Now you will finish the test on your own. Read the directions for each section carefully. Do numbers 1 through 22 just as we did the sample. Read the questions and answer choices carefully. Then darken the circle for each correct answer. When you come to the words *GO ON* at the bottom of a page, continue working on the next page. When you come to the word *STOP* at the bottom of page 27, put your pencils down. You may now begin.**

Allow students time to find and mark their answers.

S1 **A** To me, sunny days are more better

   B than rainy days because there are

   C so many things to do outside.

   D *(No mistakes)*

STOP

For questions 1–5, darken the circle for the line that has an error in the way the words are used. Darken the circle for *No mistakes* if all the words are used correctly.

1 **A** Our teacher expects us to

   B rays our hands if we have

   C something to say in class.

   D *(No mistakes)*

2 **J** "Where did you put them peanuts

   K that I brought home last night?"

   L Simeon's mother asked him.

   M *(No mistakes)*

3 **A** Mary knowed how to keep

   B secrets. She never tells anyone

   C about the things we talk about.

   D *(No mistakes)*

4 **J** Just because we don't like her

   K brother doesn't mean we

   L shouldn't go to her party.

   M *(No mistakes)*

5 **A** One of my friends brought

   B their camera to the beach

   C and took many pictures of us.

   D *(No mistakes)*

For questions 6–9, read the paragraph. Then darken the circle for each correct answer.

> [1] My sister and I like to stay overnight at our grandparents' house. [2] Grandma and Granddad take us to the movies and out to dinner. [3] At home, we hardly ever do anything exciting. [4] But the best part is bedtime so that Granddad always tells us one of his spooky stories. [5] When we go out to dinner, we can order whatever we want.

6 Which sentence does <u>not</u> belong in this paragraph?

   J Sentence 1

   K Sentence 2

   L Sentence 3

   M Sentence 5

7 Choose the best opening sentence for this paragraph.

   A My parents let me spend every weekend at my grandparents' house.

   B Sleeping at a friend's house overnight is great.

   C We always have fun when we're with our grandparents.

   D Do you ever have sleep-overs?

8 What is the best way to write the underlined part of sentence 4?

   J because Granddad

   K so that he

   L unless Granddad

   M during Granddad

9 What is the best place for sentence 5 in the paragraph?

   A Where it is now

   B Between sentences 1 and 2

   C Between sentences 3 and 4

   D After sentence 2

GO ON

Level 12

Answers
S1 ● Ⓑ Ⓒ Ⓓ   2 ● Ⓚ Ⓛ Ⓜ   4 Ⓙ Ⓚ Ⓛ ●   6 Ⓙ Ⓚ ● Ⓜ   8 ● Ⓚ Ⓛ Ⓜ
1 Ⓐ ● Ⓒ Ⓓ   3 ● Ⓑ Ⓒ Ⓓ   5 Ⓐ ● Ⓒ Ⓓ   7 Ⓐ Ⓑ ● Ⓓ   9 Ⓐ Ⓑ Ⓒ ●

25

For questions 10–15, darken the circle for the sentence or sentences that express the idea most clearly.

10   J   My favorite subjects in school are history, art, and doing experiments in science.

     K   My favorite subjects in school are history, art, and science.

     L   Learning, in school, that history, art, and science are my favorite subjects.

     M   Doing science experiments, learning history, and art are my favorite subjects in school.

11   A   Crater Lake in Oregon is the deepest lake in the United States.

     B   In the United States, Crater Lake is the deepest lake in Oregon.

     C   In Oregon, in the United States, Crater Lake is the deepest lake.

     D   Crater Lake, in the state of Oregon in the United States, is the deepest lake.

12   J   We saw silly clowns, ferocious tigers, and dancing elephants at the circus.

     K   Silly, ferocious, and dancing were the things we saw at the circus.

     L   At the circus were silly, ferocious, and dancing elephants.

     M   The silly clowns, ferocious tigers, and dancing elephants we saw at the circus.

13   A   After school, Madeleine walked and promised to take her new puppy.

     B   Promising after school, Madeleine took her new puppy for a walk.

     C   Madeleine promised to take her new puppy for a walk after school.

     D   Promising her new puppy, Madeleine took it for a walk after school.

14   J   The game wasn't exciting without knowing the players.

     K   Without knowing the players, the game wasn't exciting.

     L   The game, without knowing the players, wasn't exciting.

     M   Since we didn't know the players, the game wasn't exciting.

15   A   On Saturdays, I do chores, play basketball, and swimming.

     B   On Saturdays I do chores, play basketball, and go swimming.

     C   Swimming, playing basketball, and chores are what I do on Saturdays.

     D   Basketball, chores, and going swimming are what I do on Saturdays.

GO ON

Level 12

For questions 16–21, darken the circle for the word or words that best fit in the underlined part of the sentence. Darken the circle for *No change* if the sentence is correct as it is.

16 **Since** his favorite team wins on Sunday, my brother will be very unhappy.

   J   While
   K   Although
   L   Unless
   M   *(No change)*

17 Trish was going to let her hair grow long, **because** she decided to cut it.

   A   after
   B   but
   C   and
   D   *(No change)*

18 Monica **learned** to use a computer when she was six years old.

   J   has learned
   K   will have learned
   L   will learn
   M   *(No change)*

19 At the age of three, Dagomba boys in Africa begin learning to **drumming**.

   A   drum
   B   to drum
   C   to be drumming
   D   *(No change)*

20 **Before** he washes the dishes, Philip always soaks them in warm water.

   J   Since
   K   Until
   L   When
   M   *(No change)*

21 The weather channel just **will predict** great weather for the weekend of our camping trip.

   A   has predicted
   B   will be predicting
   C   predicted
   D   *(No change)*

For question 22, darken the circle for the paragraph that would be the most appropriate for a farewell letter to be published in a school newspaper.

22 J   Mr. Rice has been important to the math department and to everyone in our school who has had him as a teacher or a friend for the past 33 years. We have been lucky to have him for so long. Now he will have free time to spend with his grandchildren. We will miss you, Mr. Rice.

   K   Mr. Rice has been a wonderful math teacher and friend to those of us here at Lincoln School. Now he feels it's time to quit while he's ahead. Good luck, Mr. Rice. We'll miss you!

   L   It's about time that Mr. Rice retires. He's been here for too long. He's been a terrific teacher, and we all like him, but let's get a new person in here! Good luck, Mr. Rice!

   M   Mr. Rice is going to retire from Lincoln School after 33 years of service. He has taught math to children for as long as anyone can remember. Now he'd like to get away from kids for a while. We hope it's the right decision for him.

STOP

Level 12

Answers
16 Ⓙ Ⓚ ● Ⓜ   18 Ⓙ Ⓚ Ⓛ ●   20 Ⓙ Ⓚ Ⓛ ●   22 ● Ⓚ Ⓛ Ⓜ
17 Ⓐ ● Ⓒ Ⓓ   19 ● Ⓑ Ⓒ Ⓓ   21 Ⓐ Ⓑ ● Ⓓ

27

SAY: **It is now time to stop. You have completed the Unit 5 Test. Make sure that you have carefully filled in your answer spaces and have completely erased any stray marks. Then put your pencils down.**

After the test has been scored, review the questions and answer choices with students. If students are having difficulty with any lesson, provide them with additional practice items.

UNIT 6 — Math Concepts And Estimation

Lesson 10: Working with Numeration

Directions: Darken the circle for the correct answer.

> **TRY THIS** Read each question twice before choosing your answer. Be sure to think about which numbers stand for ones, tens, hundreds, and so on.

S1 Which numeral has the greatest value?

3166	3651	3561	3615	3516

A 3516   C 3615
B 3651   D 3561

> **THINK IT THROUGH** The correct answer is B. The numeral 3651, or three thousand six hundred fifty-one, has a greater value than any of the other numerals listed.

STOP

---

1 Which numeral has the same value as $\frac{17}{5}$?

A $3\frac{2}{5}$ C $5\frac{2}{3}$
B $17\frac{1}{5}$ D $1\frac{5}{12}$

2 What is the value of the 7 in 23.74?

J 7 tenths
K 7 ones
L 7 hundredths
M 7 tens

3 What should replace the ☐ in the multiplication problem shown here?

A 0
B 1
C 7
D 6

413
× 63
1239
24☐8
26 19

4 What is another way to write forty-one thousandths?

J 4.1   L 0.41
K 41,000   M 0.041

5 If 127.875 is rounded to the nearest hundredth, how would it be written?

A 127.88   C 100
B 127.9   D 200

6 What is another way to write the name for seven million, thirty thousand, two hundred nine?

J 7,030,209
K 7,030,290
L 7,300,209
M 7,030,029

STOP

Level 12

Answers

S1 Ⓐ ● Ⓒ Ⓓ   2 ● Ⓚ Ⓛ Ⓜ   4 Ⓙ Ⓚ Ⓛ ●   6 ● Ⓚ Ⓛ Ⓜ
1 ● Ⓑ Ⓒ Ⓓ   3 Ⓐ Ⓑ ● Ⓓ   5 ● Ⓑ Ⓒ Ⓓ

28

UNIT 6: Math Concepts and Estimation

Lesson 10: Working with Numeration

Mathematics Skills: Identifying place value, fractional parts, multiples of numbers; estimating; understanding number theory and relationships

SAY: **Turn to Lesson 10, Working with Numeration, on page 28.**

Check to see that all students find Lesson 10.

Distribute scratch paper to students. Tell them they may use the scratch paper to work the problems.

SAY: **In Lesson 10 you will demonstrate your understanding of number theory and number relationships.**

Read the Directions to students.

SAY: **Now look at Try This.**

Read Try This to students.

SAY: **Now look at S1. You are asked to identify which numeral has the greatest value. Look at the choices carefully. Then darken the circle for the correct answer.**

Allow students time to find and mark their answer.

SAY: **Now look at Think It Through.**

Read Think It Through to students. Check to see that all students have filled in the correct answer space. Ask students if they have any questions.

SAY: **Now you will practice answering more numeration questions. Do numbers 1 through 6 just as we did S1. When you come to the word STOP at the bottom of page 28, put your pencils down. You may now begin.**

Allow students time to find and mark their answers.

Review the questions and answer choices with students. Discuss with the class why one answer is correct and the others are not correct. Also check to see that students have carefully filled in the answer spaces and have completely erased any stray marks.

Lesson 11: Working with Number Sentences

Directions: Darken the circle for the correct answer.

TRY THIS

Only one answer will make each number sentence correct. Check each answer carefully by replacing the missing numeral with each answer choice until you obtain a correct statement.

S1 What value for ☐ makes the following number sentence correct?

A 11   C 24
B 12   D 32

THINK IT THROUGH

The correct answer is C. Test each possible answer by replacing the box in the number sentence with each answer choice. By doing this, you will see that 24 is the only numeral that makes the number sentence correct.

STOP

1 Which numeral will make this number sentence true?

A 9   C 6
B 3   D 2

2 Which numeral would replace the ☐ to make the number sentence true?

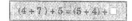

J 7   L 5
K 4   M 0

3 What would replace the ☐ to make the fractions equivalent?

A 6   C 1
B 11   D 2

4 What value for ☐ will make the following number sentence true?

J 6   L 2
K 4   M 1

5 What would replace the ☐ in the number sentence $54 - (46 - 10) + 6 = $ ☐?

A −10   C 6
B 34   D 24

6 What would replace the ☐ to make the fractions equivalent?

J 3   L 5
K 4   M 2

STOP

Level 12

Answers
S1 Ⓐ Ⓑ ● Ⓓ   2 ● Ⓚ Ⓛ Ⓜ   4 Ⓙ Ⓚ ● Ⓜ   6 Ⓙ ● Ⓛ Ⓜ
1 Ⓐ ● Ⓒ Ⓓ   3 ● Ⓑ Ⓒ Ⓓ   5 Ⓐ Ⓑ Ⓒ ●

29

Lesson 11: Working with Number Sentences

Mathematics Skill: Solving number sentences

SAY: **Turn to Lesson 11, Working with Number Sentences, on page 29.**

Check to see that all students find Lesson 11.

Distribute scratch paper to students. Tell them they may use the scratch paper to work the problems.

SAY: **In Lesson 11 you will practice solving number sentences.**

Read the Directions to students.

SAY: **Now look at Try This.**

Read Try This to students.

SAY: **Now look at S1. You are asked to identify the missing numeral that would make the number sentence correct. Look at the choices carefully. Then darken the circle for the correct answer.**

Allow students time to find and mark their answer.

SAY: **Now look at Think It Through.**

Read Think It Through to students. Check to see that all students have filled in the correct answer space. Ask students if they have any questions.

SAY: **Now you will practice solving more number sentences. Do numbers 1 through 6 just as we did S1. When you come to the word STOP at the bottom of page 29, put your pencils down. You may now begin.**

Allow students time to find and mark their answers.

Review the questions and answer choices with students. Discuss with the class why one answer is correct and the others are not correct. Also check to see that students have carefully filled in the answer spaces and have completely erased any stray marks.

Lesson 12: Using Measurement and Geometry

Directions: Darken the circle for the correct answer.

TRY THIS   Use the objects shown or named to help you answer each question.

S1 A window ledge is 7 feet above the ground. **Which of the following describes the distance of the ledge from the ground?**

A   Between 1 and 2 yards

B   Less than 1 yard

C   Greater than 3 yards

D   Between 2 and 3 yards

THINK IT THROUGH   The correct answer is D. Since there are 3 feet in a yard, and $7 \div 3 = 2\frac{1}{3}$ the correct answer is <u>between 2 and 3 yards.</u>

STOP

---

1 Which figure shown here is <u>not</u> a trapezoid?

A   C

B   D

2 Which unit of measurement is best to use to describe the weight of a sack of potatoes?

J   Feet   L   Liters

K   Ounces   M   Pounds

3 The figure shown here has $\frac{3}{10}$ of its area shaded. **How much is <u>not</u> shaded?**

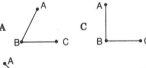

A $\frac{1}{2}$ C $\frac{3}{7}$

B $\frac{7}{10}$ D $\frac{3}{10}$

4 In the congruent figures shown here, which part of the second figure corresponds to $\overline{BC}$?

J $\overline{NO}$ L $\overline{PQ}$

K $\overline{MN}$ M $\overline{OP}$

5 Which angle is greater than 90°?

6 What is a reasonable estimate of the length of a bicycle?

J   4 meters   L   100 centimeters

K   5 feet   M   3 yards

STOP

Level 12

Answers

30

S1 Ⓐ Ⓑ Ⓒ ●   2 Ⓙ Ⓚ Ⓛ ●   4 ● Ⓚ Ⓛ Ⓜ   6 Ⓙ ● Ⓛ Ⓜ

1 Ⓐ Ⓑ ● Ⓓ   3 Ⓐ ● Ⓒ Ⓓ   5 Ⓐ ● Ⓒ Ⓓ

Lesson 12: Using Measurement and Geometry

Mathematics Skills: Working with customary and metric units of length; identifying congruent and similar figures; recognizing three-dimensional forms; identifying angles and line segments; estimating

SAY: **Turn to Lesson 12, Using Measurement and Geometry, on page 30.**

Check to see that all students find Lesson 12.

Distribute scratch paper to students. Tell them they may use the scratch paper to work the problems.

SAY: **In Lesson 12 you will practice solving problems about measurement and shape.**

Read the <u>Directions</u> to students.

SAY: **Now look at <u>Try This</u>.**

Read <u>Try This</u> to students.

SAY: **Now look at S1. You are asked to find the distance a window ledge is from the ground. Read the answer choices carefully. Then darken the circle for the correct answer.**

Allow students time to find and mark their answer.

SAY: **Now look at <u>Think It Through</u>.**

Read <u>Think It Through</u> to students. Check to see that all students have filled in the correct answer space. Ask students if they have any questions.

SAY: **Now you will practice solving more problems about measurement and shape. Do numbers 1 through 6 just as we did S1. When you come to the word *STOP* at the bottom of page 30, put your pencils down. You may now begin.**

Allow students time to find and mark their answers.

Review the questions and answer choices with students. Discuss with the class why one answer is correct and the others are not correct. Also check to see that students have carefully filled in the answer spaces and have completely erased any stray marks.

Lesson 13: Working with Probability and Statistics

Directions: Darken the circle for the correct answer.

TRY THIS
To find the average (mean) of a set of numbers, first add the numbers. Then divide the sum by the number of addends in the set.

S1 What is the average (mean) of this set of numbers {10, 9, 14, 11}?

A 44

B 55

C 11

D 9

THINK IT THROUGH
The correct answer is C. The sum of the set of numbers is 44, and 44 ÷ 4 = 11.

STOP

---

1 Which number is needed in this set {61, 40, 58, □} so that the average (mean) is 49?

A 37

B 21

C 49

D 47

2 What is the average (mean) of the set {25, 37, 16, 30}?

J 27

K 108

L 21.6

M 36

3 Which set of numbers shown here has the greatest average (mean)?

A {3, 5, 7}

B {1, 9, 2}

C {9, 4, 5}

D {5, 5, 5}

4 If Ike spins the spinner, on which number is it most likely to stop?

J 1

K 2

L 3

M 4

5 For which of the following does a mean (average) not make sense?

A Weekly allowance received by eight sixth graders

B Books read by one sixth-grade student last month

C Five quiz scores in math

D High temperature during the past four days

6 Which set of numbers shown here has the greatest average (mean)?

J {12, 19, 20}

K {17, 19, 15}

L {24, 20, 10}

M {20, 15, 16}

STOP

Answers

S1 Ⓐ Ⓑ ● Ⓓ   2 ● Ⓚ Ⓛ Ⓜ   4 ● Ⓚ Ⓛ Ⓜ   6 Ⓙ Ⓚ ● Ⓜ

1 ● Ⓑ Ⓒ Ⓓ   3 Ⓐ Ⓑ ● Ⓓ   5 Ⓐ ● Ⓒ Ⓓ

Lesson 13: Working with Probability and Statistics

Mathematics Skills: Understanding probability and statistics concepts and their application in problem solving

SAY: **Turn to Lesson 13, Working with Probability and Statistics, on page 31.**

Check to see that all students find Lesson 13.

Distribute scratch paper to students. Tell them they may use the scratch paper to work the problems.

SAY: **In Lesson 13 you will practice solving problems of probability and statistics.**

Read the Directions to students.

SAY: **Now look at Try This.**

Read Try This to students.

SAY: **Now look at S1. You are asked to find the average of four numbers. Find the solution. Then darken the circle for the correct answer.**

Allow students time to find and mark their answer.

SAY: **Now look at Think It Through.**

Read Think It Through to students. Check to see that all students have filled in the correct answer space. Ask students if they have any questions.

SAY: **Now you will practice solving more problems of probability and statistics. Do numbers 1 through 6 just as we did S1. When you come to the word *STOP* at the bottom of page 31, put your pencils down. You may now begin.**

Allow students time to find and mark their answers.

Review the questions and answer choices with students. Discuss with the class why one answer is correct and the others are not correct. Also check to see that students have carefully filled in the answer spaces and have completely erased any stray marks.

Lesson 14: Understanding Mathematical Relations

Directions: Darken the circle for the correct answer.

TRY THIS
Read each problem very carefully. Try using all the answer choices back in the problem. Then choose the answer that you think best answers the question.

S1 If $y + 13 = 25$, what is the value of y?

A 7
B 12
C 24
D 38

THINK IT THROUGH
The correct answer is B. Subtract 13 from both sides of the equation, and $y = 25 - 13 = 12$.

STOP

1 Which inequality is represented on the number line shown here?

3

A $x < 3$
B $x > 3$
C $x \leq 3$
D $x \geq 3$

2 The numbers in the two boxes shown here are formed by the same rule. **What number is missing?**

0, 1, 3, 6, 10, 15, 21
2, 3, 5, 8, ☐, 17

J 11
K 12
L 13
M 14

3 Which number line represents $x < 5$?

A
2 3 4 5 6 7 8 9

B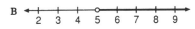
2 3 4 5 6 7 8 9

C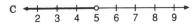
2 3 4 5 6 7 8 9

D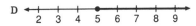
2 3 4 5 6 7 8 9

4 What is the value of x if $\frac{x}{3} = 12$?

J 4
K 9
L 15
M 36

STOP

Level 12

Answers

S1 Ⓐ ● Ⓒ Ⓓ   2 Ⓙ ● Ⓛ Ⓜ   4 Ⓙ Ⓚ Ⓛ ●
1 Ⓐ Ⓑ Ⓒ ●   3 Ⓐ Ⓑ ● Ⓓ

32

Lesson 14: Understanding Mathematical Relations

Mathematics Skills: Describing and representing relationships; working with variables, equations, and number patterns

SAY: **Turn to Lesson 14, Understanding Mathematical Relations, on page 32.**

Check to see that all students find Lesson 14.

Distribute scratch paper to students. Tell them they may use the scratch paper to work the problems.

SAY: **In Lesson 14 you will practice solving problems using variables, equations, and number patterns.**

Read the Directions to students.

SAY: **Now look at Try This.**

Read Try This to students.

SAY: **Now look at S1. You are asked to find the value of a variable in an equation. Read the answer choices carefully. Then darken the circle for the correct answer.**

Allow students time to find and mark their answer.

SAY: **Now look at Think It Through.**

Read Think It Through to students. Check to see that all students have filled in the correct answer space. Ask students if they have any questions.

SAY: **Now you will practice solving more problems using variables and equations, and solving number patterns. Do numbers 1 through 4 just as we did S1. When you come to the word STOP at the bottom of page 32, put your pencils down. You may now begin.**

Allow students time to find and mark their answers.

Review the questions and answer choices with students. Discuss with the class why one answer is correct and the others are not correct. Also check to see that students have carefully filled in the answer spaces and have completely erased any stray marks.

Lesson 15: Using Estimation

Directions: Darken the circle for the correct answer.

| TRY THIS | When you estimate answers, round the numbers so that only the first digit is not zero. |

S1 The closest estimate of 52×27 is _____.

A 1,500   C 1,800

B 1,000   D 1,200

| THINK IT THROUGH | The correct answer is A. Round 52 to 50, and round 27 to 30. $50 \times 30 = \underline{1,500}$. |

STOP

---

1 The closest estimate of $22 \div 7\frac{1}{12}$ is _____.

A 2   C 4

B 3   D 15

2 The closest estimate of the total weight of the two bricks is _____.

3.89 pounds   5.25 pounds

J 7 pounds   L 9 pounds

K 8 pounds   M 10 pounds

3 The closest estimate of $\$18.34 - \$3.28$ is _____.

A $16   C $14

B $15   D $13

4 The closest estimate of $1,826 \div 8$ is between _____.

J 100 and 200

K 200 and 300

L 300 and 400

M 400 and 500

5 The closest estimate of $35,103 \div 7$ is _____.

A 5,000   C 50

B 500   D 50,000

6 The closest estimate of the cost of the cereal is _____.

Total cost is $4.97.

Cereal ?

Milk $1.99

J $3   L $300

K $30   M $3000

STOP

Level 12

Answers

S1 ● Ⓑ Ⓒ Ⓓ   2 Ⓙ Ⓚ ● Ⓜ   4 Ⓙ ● Ⓛ Ⓜ   6 ● Ⓚ Ⓛ Ⓜ

1 Ⓐ ● Ⓒ Ⓓ   3 Ⓐ ● Ⓒ Ⓓ   5 ● Ⓑ Ⓒ Ⓓ

33

Lesson 15: Using Estimation

Mathematics Skill: Estimating

SAY: **Turn to Lesson 15, Using Estimation, on page 33.**

Check to see that all students find Lesson 15.

Do not distribute scratch paper to students. Tell them they should work the estimation problems in their heads.

SAY: **In Lesson 15 you will practice estimating answers to problems.**

Read the Directions to students.

SAY: **Now look at Try This.**

Read Try This to students.

SAY: **Now look at S1. You are asked to estimate the answer to a multiplication problem. Read the answer choices carefully. Then darken the circle for the correct answer.**

Allow students time to find and mark their answer.

SAY: **Now look at Think It Through.**

Read Think It Through to students. Check to see that all students have filled in the correct answer space. Ask students if they have any questions.

SAY: **Now you will practice estimating answers to more problems. Do numbers 1 through 6 just as we did S1. When you come to the word STOP at the bottom of page 33, put your pencils down. You may now begin.**

Allow students time to find and mark their answers.

Review the questions and answer choices with students. Discuss with the class why one answer is correct and the others are not correct. Also check to see that students have carefully filled in the answer spaces and have completely erased any stray marks.

Unit 6 Test

S1 What is the value of the 5 in 31.65?

   A 5 tenths

   B 5 ones

   C 5 hundredths

   D 5 tens

STOP

For questions 1–33, darken the circle for the correct answer.

1 Which numeral has the greatest value?

5467	6745	7564	4567	7654

   A 4567   C 6745

   B 7654   D 7564

2 What is another way to write eighty-three thousandths?

   J 0.83   L 83,000

   K 0.083   M 8.3

3 What should replace the ☐ in the multiplication problem shown here?

   A 0

   B 5

   C 6

   D 7

$$\begin{array}{r} 217 \\ \times\ 54 \\ \hline 868 \\ 108\square \\ \hline 117\triangle 8 \end{array}$$

4 Which is another way to write 3×10^4?

   J $3 \times \frac{4}{10}$

   K $3 \times 10 \times 10 \times 10 \times 10$

   L $3 \times 10 \times 4$

   M $3 \times \frac{10}{4}$

5 If 346.786 is rounded to the nearest hundredth, how would it be written?

   A 346.79

   B 346.78

   C 346.8

   D 300

6 What is another way to write the name for two million, thirteen thousand, one hundred five?

   J 2,130,015

   K 2,130,105

   L 2,013,105

   M 2,013,150

7 What is the greatest common factor of 6 and 24?

   A 6   C 3

   B 2   D 30

8 Which numeral has the same value as $\frac{13}{5}$?

   J $2\frac{3}{5}$ L $\frac{5}{13}$

   K $1\frac{3}{5}$ M $3\frac{2}{5}$

9 Which numeral has the same value as $\frac{34}{8}$?

   A $3\frac{1}{2}$ C $4\frac{1}{4}$

   B $4\frac{1}{2}$ D $3\frac{3}{4}$

GO ON

Level 12

Answers

34

S1 Ⓐ Ⓑ ● Ⓓ   2 Ⓙ ● Ⓛ Ⓜ   4 Ⓙ ● Ⓛ Ⓜ   6 Ⓙ Ⓚ ● Ⓜ   8 ● Ⓚ Ⓛ Ⓜ

1 Ⓐ ● Ⓒ Ⓓ   3 Ⓐ ● Ⓒ Ⓓ   5 ● Ⓑ Ⓒ Ⓓ   7 ● Ⓑ Ⓒ Ⓓ   9 Ⓐ Ⓑ ● Ⓓ

Unit 6 Test

SAY: **Turn to the Unit 6 Test on page 34.**

Check to see that all students find the Unit 6 Test.

Distribute scratch paper to students. Tell them they may use the scratch paper to work all problems except numbers 30 through 33 on page 37. These are estimation problems that students should work in their heads.

SAY: **In this test you will use the mathematics skills that we have practiced in this unit. Look at S1. You are asked to find the value of _5_ in the number _31.65_. Darken the circle for the correct answer.**

Allow students time to find and mark their answer.

SAY: **You should have darkened the circle for _C_ because the _5_ is in the hundredths place.**

Check to see that all students have filled in the correct answer space. Ask students if they have any questions.

SAY: **Now you will finish the test on your own. Do numbers 1 through 33 just as we did S1. Read the problems and answer choices carefully. Then darken the circle for each correct answer. When you come to the words _GO ON_ at the bottom of a page, continue working on the next page. When you come to the word _STOP_ at the bottom of page 37, put your pencils down. You may now begin.**

Allow students time to find and mark their answers.

Unit 6 Test

S1 What is the value of the 5 in 31.65?

   A 5 tenths

   B 5 ones

   C 5 hundredths

   D 5 tens

STOP

For questions 1–33, darken the circle for the correct answer.

1 Which numeral has the greatest value?

5467	6745	7564	4567	7654

   A 4567   **C** 6745

   B 7654   **D** 7564

2 What is another way to write eighty-three thousandths?

   J 0.83   **L** 83,000

   K 0.083   **M** 8.3

3 What should replace the □ in the multiplication problem shown here?

   A 0

   B 5

   C 6

   D 7

$$
\begin{array}{r}
217 \\
\times\ 54 \\
\hline
868 \\
108\square \\
\hline
117\triangle8
\end{array}
$$

4 Which is another way to write 3×10^4?

   J $3 \times \frac{4}{10}$

   K $3 \times 10 \times 10 \times 10 \times 10$

   L $3 \times 10 \times 4$

   M $3 \times \frac{10}{4}$

5 If 346.786 is rounded to the nearest hundredth, how would it be written?

   A 346.79

   B 346.78

   C 346.8

   D 300

6 What is another way to write the name for two million, thirteen thousand, one hundred five?

   J 2,130,015

   K 2,130,105

   L 2,013,105

   M 2,013,150

7 What is the greatest common factor of 6 and 24?

   A 6   **C** 3

   B 2   **D** 30

8 Which numeral has the same value as $\frac{13}{5}$?

   J $2\frac{3}{5}$ **L** $\frac{5}{13}$

   K $1\frac{3}{5}$ **M** $3\frac{2}{5}$

9 Which numeral has the same value as $\frac{34}{8}$?

   A $3\frac{1}{2}$ **C** $4\frac{1}{4}$

   B $4\frac{1}{2}$ **D** $3\frac{3}{4}$

GO ON

Level 12

10 Which numeral will make the number sentence true?

$$(6 \times \square) + 3 = 27$$

J 6

K 3

L 5

M 4

11 Which numeral would replace the $\square$ to make the number sentence true?

$$(3 + 6) + 8 = (8 + 3) + \square$$

A 3

B 8

C 0

D 6

12 What would replace the $\square$ to make the fractions equivalent?

$$\frac{7}{10} = \frac{\square}{30}$$

J 21

K 3

L 210

M 28

13 What would replace the $\square$ in the number sentence $65 - (42 - 9) + 8 = \square$?

A 18

B 40

C 22

D 24

14 Which figure below is <u>not</u> a rectangle?

J   **L**

K   **M**

15 Which unit of measurement is best to use to describe the weight of a box of cereal?

A Inches

B Ounces

C Pounds

D Meters

16 The figure shown here has $\frac{3}{8}$ of its area shaded. **How much is <u>not</u> shaded?**

J $\frac{5}{8}$ **L** $\frac{3}{5}$

K $\frac{1}{2}$ **M** $\frac{7}{8}$

17 On a map of a hiking trail, l inch represents 3 miles. **What is the length of the trail if the distance from the beginning to the turnaround is 3 inches?**

A 6 miles

B 9 miles

C 12 miles

D 3 miles

GO ON

Level 12

Answers

10 Ⓙ Ⓚ Ⓛ ●   **12** ● Ⓚ Ⓛ Ⓜ   **14** Ⓙ Ⓚ Ⓛ ●   **16** ● Ⓚ Ⓛ Ⓜ

11 Ⓐ Ⓑ Ⓒ ●   **13** ● Ⓑ Ⓒ Ⓓ   **15** Ⓐ ● Ⓒ Ⓓ   **17** Ⓐ ● Ⓒ Ⓓ

35

18 What is a reasonable estimate of the width of a doorway?

J 1 meter

K 7 feet

L 50 centimeters

M 3 yards

19 In the congruent figures shown here, which part of the second figure corresponds to $\overline{CD}$?

A $\overline{JK}$ **C** $\overline{KL}$

B $\overline{JM}$ **D** $\overline{LM}$

20 Which circle will fit within a 5-inch square and have the least amount of the square remain uncovered?

21 What is another way to write 72 seconds?

A 1 minute 12 seconds

B 1.12 minutes

C 0.72 minutes

D 7.2 minutes

22 On a map of a bike trail, 1 inch represents 4 miles. **What is the length of the trail if the distance from the south end to the north end is 5 inches?**

J 10 miles

K 8 miles

L 9 miles

M 20 miles

23 For which of the following does a mean (average) of the students in your math class not make sense?

A The height of your classmates

B The weight of your classmates

C The color of your classmates' eyes

D The number of minutes spent doing homework yesterday

24 What is the average (mean) of these numbers {79, 89, 94, 88, 95}?

J 85   **L** 425

K 89   **M** 445

25 Kim's favorite word game uses the spinner shown here. **When Kim takes a turn, at which letter will the spinner most likely stop?**

A N

B S

C B

D A

GO ON

26 What is the value of x if $\frac{x}{5} = 20$?

J 4 L 15

K 100 M 25

27 Which number line shows $x > 3$?

A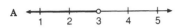

B

C

D

28 The numbers in the two boxes shown here are formed by the same rule. **What number is missing?**

| 2, 3, 5, 8, 12, 17 |

| 1, 2, 4, 7, ☐, 16 |

J 11 L 13

K 12 M 14

29 Which inequality is shown on this number line?

5

A $x < 5$ C $x \le 5$

B $x > 5$ D $x \ge 5$

30 The closest estimate of the time remaining until the race is _____.

Race time is 10:02 A.M.

Time now is 7:54 A.M.

J 1 hour L 3 hours

K 2 hours M 4 hours

31 The closest estimate of 246×560 is _____.

A 300×600

B 200×600

C 200×500

D 300×500

32 The closest estimate of the cost of 22 packs of gum is _____.

1 pack of gum for 47¢.

J $0.10 L $10.00

K $1.00 M $100.00

33 The closest estimate of $4.23 + 3.16 + 6.91$ is _____.

A 14 C 1.4

B 13 D 1,400

STOP

Level 12

37

Answers

26 J ● L M   28 ● K L M   30 J ● L M   32 J K ● M

27 A B C ●   29 A B ● D   31 A ● C D   33 ● B C D

SAY: **It is now time to stop. You have completed the Unit 6 Test. Make sure that you have carefully filled in your answer spaces and have completely erased any stray marks. Then put your pencils down.**

After the test has been scored, review the questions and answer choices with students. If students are having difficulty, provide them with additional practice items.

UNIT 7 Math Problems

Lesson 16: Solving Problems

Directions: Darken the circle for the correct answer. Darken the circle for Not given if the correct answer is not shown.

TRY THIS

Read each problem carefully. Then decide how to find the correct answer.

S1 Julio can save $12 a week from his allowance and paper route. **How much money will he have saved after 6 weeks?**

A $6   C $72

B $18   D Not given

THINK IT THROUGH

The correct answer is C. To find how much money Julio will have saved after 6 weeks, multiply the amount of money he saves in one week by 6 weeks. So, 12 x 6 = the amount.

STOP

1 Jake runs both the 1500-meter race and the 800-meter race. **How many meters does he run altogether?**

A 700   C 2300

B 2200   D Not given

2 The school cafeteria sells sandwiches on whole wheat or white bread, made with turkey, beef, chicken, or tuna fish. **How many different combinations are possible?**

J 2   L 6

K 4   M 8

3 Aldo bought 6 greeting cards. Two of them were $3 each and the rest were $2 each. **How can Aldo figure out exactly how much the greeting cards cost?**

A Multiply 2 times $3, and add this amount to 2 times $2.

B Multiply 2 times $3, and add this amount to 3 times $2.

C Multiply 6 times $3.

D Multiply 2 times $3, and add this amount to 4 times $2

4 Kenny needs 9 cups of juice concentrate for the cooler. **How can he figure out how many times he needs to fill the $\frac{1}{2}$-cup measure to get 9 cups?**

J Divide 9 by $\frac{1}{2}$

K Multiply 9 by $\frac{1}{2}$

L Subtract $\frac{1}{2}$ from 9

M Add 9 and $\frac{1}{2}$

5 One fourth of the students in Mrs. Scanlon's class ride their bikes to school. There are 7 bike riders in the class. **How many students are in the class?**

A 7   C 28

B 11   D Not given

6 Mr. and Mrs. Sessler and their children, John and Jessica, went to the basketball game. The total cost for two adult tickets was $6.50. The children's tickets cost $1.00 each. Mr. Sessler gave the cashier $10.00. **How much change did Mr. Sessler receive?**

J $1.00   L $2.50

K $1.50   M Not given

GO ON
Level 12

Answers

S1 ⓐ ⓑ ● ⓓ   2 ⓙ ⓚ ⓛ ●   4 ⓙ ● ⓛ Ⓜ   6 ⓙ ● ⓛ Ⓜ

1 ⓐ ⓑ ● ⓓ   3 ⓐ ⓑ ⓒ ●   5 ⓐ ⓑ ● ⓓ

38

Mathematics Skills: Solving word problems by using addition, subtraction, multiplication, and division of whole numbers, fractions, and decimals

SAY: **Turn to Lesson 16, Solving Problems, on page 38.**

Check to see that all students find Lesson 16.

SAY: **In Lesson 16 you will practice solving word problems.**

Read the Directions to students.

SAY: **Now look at Try This.**

Read Try This to students.

SAY: **Now look at S1. Read the problem carefully. Decide how to find the correct answer. Work the problem, then darken the circle for the correct answer. Darken the circle for *Not given* if the correct answer is not given.**

Allow students time to find and mark their answer.

SAY: **Now look at Think It Through.**

Read Think It Through to students. Check to see that all students have filled in the correct answer space. Ask students if they have any questions.

SAY: **Now you will practice solving more word problems. Do numbers 1 through 12 just as we did S1. When you go to the words *GO ON* at the bottom of page 38, continue working on the next page. When you come to the word *STOP* at the bottom of page 39, put your pencils down. You may now begin.**

Allow students time to find and mark their answers.

Car Care Center

CLEANING SERVICES

Service	Cars	Trucks/Vans
Wash	$2.50	$3.50
Wax	$2.00	$3.00
Floormats washed	$0.75 ea	$0.75 ea
Interior vacuumed	$2.00	$2.25
Dashboard cleaned	$1.50	$1.50
Tires/wheels polished	$1.00/set	$1.00/set
Special I	$5.00	$7.00
Special II	$8.25	$10.50

CUSTOM SERVICES

Pin striping	$1.90 per 2 feet
Window tinting	$6.35 per foot
Painting (labor)	$35.00 per hour
Repairs (labor)	$42.00 per hour

For questions 7–12, use the picture shown here. Do not add sales tax.

7 Gene took his car to Car Care Center. He asked for the Special I which included a wash, wax, and interior vacuum. **How much money did he save by getting the Special I instead of having each service performed separately?**

A $1.50 C $1.00

B $1.25 D Not given

8 Jamal and Marita took their mother's car to Car Care Center. They had the car washed, the interior vacuumed, and the dashboard cleaned. They shared the cost equally. **How much money did each pay?**

J $3.50 L $3.00

K $3.25 M Not given

9 How much should Han pay for $2\frac{1}{2}$ hours of labor for painting his car?

A $70.00 C $87.50

B $88.50 D Not given

10 Elizabeth took the family van to Car Care Center and had it washed and waxed. She gave the attendant $20. **How much change did she receive?**

J $15.50 L $13.50

K $16.00 M Not given

11 Mr. Lutz took his van to Car Care Center to have some pin striping done on the door panels. There was a total of 6.2 feet of pin striping. **About how much did the pin striping cost?**

A $2.00 C $8.00

B $6.00 D $10.00

12 It took 6.75 hours to repair Eileen's car. **How much did she pay for labor on the repairs?**

J $157.25 L $299.35

K $283.50 M $416.00

STOP

Level 12

Answers
7 ● Ⓑ Ⓒ Ⓓ   9 Ⓐ Ⓑ ● Ⓓ   11 Ⓐ ● Ⓒ Ⓓ
8 Ⓙ Ⓚ ● Ⓜ   10 Ⓙ Ⓚ ● Ⓜ   12 Ⓙ ● Ⓛ Ⓜ

39

Lesson 17: Working with Graphs and Tables

Directions: Darken the circle for the correct answer.

┌─────┐
│ TRY │   Study the graph or table carefully. Look for key words or numbers in the
│THIS │   question that tell you what to look for in the table or graph.
└─────┘

S1

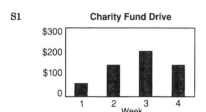

Charity Fund Drive

The graph shows the weekly totals for the Student Council Charity Fund Drive. The goal was to raise $500. **During which week did the students reach the halfway mark toward their goal?**

A   Week 1

B   Week 2

C   Week 3

D   Week 4

┌──────────┐
│ **THINK**│ The correct answer is C. The halfway mark toward the goal of $500 is
│ **IT**   │ $250. During the first two weeks, the students raised a total of $200.
│**THROUGH**│ During the third week, they raised $200. Since $200 and $200 = $400,
└──────────┘ the students reached the halfway mark toward their goal sometime during the third week.

STOP

Use the graph to answer questions 1–3.

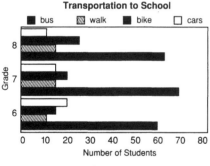

Transportation to School

■ bus   ▨ walk   ■ bike   □ cars

Grade / Number of Students

1   **How many sixth-grade students ride the bus to school?**

A   60   C   70

B   65   D   105

2   **How many students altogether walk or ride their bikes to school?**

J   25

K   35

L   40

M   100

3   **Which grade has the least number of students?**

A   Grade 6

B   Grade 7

C   Grade 8

D   Grades 6 and 7 have the same number.

GO ON

Level 12

Answers

S1 ⓐ ⓑ ● ⓓ   2 ⓙ ⓚ ⓛ ●

40   1 ● ⓑ ⓒ ⓓ   3 ● ⓑ ⓒ ⓓ

Lesson 17: Working with Graphs and Tables

Mathematics Skills: Interpreting graphs and tables; evaluating graphic displays and using the information to solve problems

SAY: **Turn to Lesson 17, Working with Graphs and Tables, on page 40.**

Check to see that all students find Lesson 17.

SAY: **In Lesson 17 you will practice interpreting information presented in graphic form and using the information to solve problems.**

Read the Directions to students.

SAY: **Now look at Try This.**

Read Try This to students.

SAY: **Now look at S1. Read the problem and study the graph carefully. Then darken the circle for the correct answer.**

Allow students time to find and mark their answer.

SAY: **Now look at Think It Through.**

Read Think It Through to students. Check to see that all students have filled in the correct answer space. Ask students if they have any questions.

SAY: **Now you will practice interpreting more graphs and tables. Do numbers 1 through 9 just as we did S1. When you come to the words _GO ON_ at the bottom of page 40, continue working on the next page. When you come to the word _STOP_ at the bottom of page 41, put your pencils down. You may now begin.**

Allow students time to find and mark their answers.

Lesson 17: Working with Graphs and Tables

Directions: Darken the circle for the correct answer.

TRY THIS | Study the graph or table carefully. Look for key words or numbers in the question that tell you what to look for in the table or graph.

S1

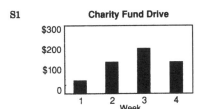

Charity Fund Drive

The graph shows the weekly totals for the Student Council Charity Fund Drive. The goal was to raise $500. **During which week did the students reach the halfway mark toward their goal?**

A   Week 1

B   Week 2

C   Week 3

D   Week 4

THINK IT THROUGH | The correct answer is <u>C</u>. The halfway mark toward the goal of $500 is $250. During the first two weeks, the students raised a total of $200. During the third week, they raised $200. Since $200 and $200 = $400, the students reached the halfway mark toward their goal sometime during the third week.

STOP

Use the graph to answer questions 1–3.

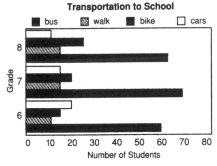

Transportation to School

■ bus   ▨ walk   ■ bike   □ cars

Grade / Number of Students

1   How many sixth-grade students ride the bus to school?

A   60   C   70

B   65   D   105

2   How many students altogether walk or ride their bikes to school?

J   25

K   35

L   40

M   100

3   Which grade has the least number of students?

A   Grade 6

B   Grade 7

C   Grade 8

D   Grades 6 and 7 have the same number.

GO ON

Level 12

Answers

S1 Ⓐ Ⓑ ● Ⓓ   2 Ⓙ Ⓚ Ⓛ ●

40

1 ● Ⓑ Ⓒ Ⓓ   3 ● Ⓑ Ⓒ Ⓓ

This table below lists the prices of art supplies. Study the table. Then answer questions 4–6.

Art Supplies		
	each	10-pack
tablet	$1.20	$10.00
chalk	$2.00	$18.00
markers	$3.25	$30.00
crayons	$1.50	$12.00
paint	$2.50	$20.00
scissors	$3.00	$25.00
glue	$0.75	$6.00
tissue paper	$2.25	$20.00
construction paper	$2.00	$18.00

4 Which of the following groups of items could be purchased with $5.00?

  J Chalk, paint, and crayons

  K Construction paper, glue, and markers

  L Paint, glue, and a tablet

  M Scissors, chalk, and glue

5 How much would 1 individual package of markers, crayons, and chalk cost altogether?

  A $6.00   **C** $6.50

  B $6.25   **D** $6.75

6 An art teacher is buying paints for 99 students. Which of these is the best buy?

  J 99 single pack

  K 10 packs of 10

  L 9 packs of 10 and 9 single packs

  M 8 packs of 10 and 19 single packs

Use the graph shown here to answer questions 7–9.

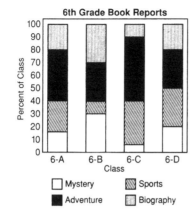

6th Grade Book Reports

7 About what percent of class 6-A did **not** read biographies?

  A 30%

  B 40%

  C 60%

  D 80%

8 About what percent of class 6-C read adventure books?

  J 5%

  K 30%

  L 40%

  M 50%

9 In class 6-B, which kinds of books were read by the same percent of the class?

  A Mystery and sports

  B Sports and adventure

  C Mystery, biography, and adventure

  D Sports and biography

STOP

Level 12

41

Answers

4 Ⓙ Ⓚ ● Ⓜ   **6** Ⓙ ● Ⓛ Ⓜ   **8** Ⓙ Ⓚ Ⓛ ●

5 Ⓐ Ⓑ Ⓒ ●   **7** Ⓐ Ⓑ Ⓒ ●   **9** Ⓐ Ⓑ ● Ⓓ

Review the questions and answer choices with students. Discuss with the class why one answer is correct and the others are not correct. Also check to see that students have carefully filled in the answer spaces and have completely erased any stray marks.

S1 Michael walked once around the track at the high school in 2 minutes. **How many times can he walk around it in 16 minutes?**

A 8

B 14

C 18

D 32

STOP

For questions 1–20, darken the circle for the correct answer. Darken the circle for Not given if the correct answer is not shown.

Use the table below to answer questions 1–4.

Museum Snack-Bar Menu	
Hot dog	$1.25
Hamburger	$1.50
Grilled cheese	$1.50
Pizza (slice)	$1.75
Turkey sandwich	$2.25
Milk	$0.50
Juice	$0.60
Chips	$0.50
Fries	$0.75
Cookies	$1.00
Ice-cream cup	$0.75
Fresh fruit	$0.50

1 How much did Nick pay for a pizza slice, juice, and cookies?

A $2.35   C $3.45

B $3.35   D $4.35

2 How much more does an order of a hamburger, fries, juice, and an ice-cream cup cost than an order of grilled cheese, chips, and milk?

J $1.10   L $3.60

K $2.50   M $6.10

3 Mr. and Mrs. Chen bought lunch for themselves and their two children. **How much did they pay altogether for 1 hamburger, 1 bag of chips, 1 milk, and 1 package of cookies for each of them?**

A $3.50

B $12.50

C $14.00

D Not given

4 Billy and Bobby split the cost of 5 hot dogs, and 3 orders of fries. **How much did they each pay?**

J $2.00

K $4.00

L $4.25

M $8.50

5 Jesse puts postcards into an album. Each album page has room for 4 postcards. **How many pages does he need for his collection of 78 postcards?**

A 12

B 19

C 20

D 21

6 Party plates are on sale for 2 packs for $3.00. Each pack contains 8 plates. **How many plates did Tracy get for $6.00?**

J 2

K 4

L 16

M 32

GO ON

Level 12

Answers

S1 ● Ⓑ Ⓒ Ⓓ   **2** ● Ⓚ Ⓛ Ⓜ   **4** Ⓙ Ⓚ ● Ⓜ   **6** Ⓙ Ⓚ Ⓛ ●

1 Ⓐ ● Ⓒ Ⓓ   **3** Ⓐ Ⓑ ● Ⓓ   **5** Ⓐ Ⓑ ● Ⓓ

42

Unit 7 Test

Distribute scratch paper to students. Tell them to compute their answers on the scratch paper.

SAY: **Turn to the Unit 7 Test on page 42.**

Check to see that all students find the Unit 7 Test.

SAY: **In this test you will use the mathematics skills that we have practiced in this unit. We will work the sample together before you begin the test. Look at S1. Read the problem carefully. You are asked to find how many times Michael can walk around the track in 16 minutes. Darken the circle for the correct answer.**

Allow students time to find and mark their answer.

SAY: **You should have darkened the circle for A. If Michael walks around the track once in 2 minutes, in 16 minutes Michael could walk around the track 8 times. You divide 16 by 2 to get the correct answer.**

Check to see that all students have filled in the correct answer space. Ask students if they have any questions.

SAY: **Now you will finish the test on your own. Do numbers 1 through 20 just as we did the sample. Read the questions and answer choices carefully. Then darken the circle for each correct answer. When you come to the words *GO ON* at the bottom of a page, continue working on the next page. When you come to the word *STOP* at the bottom of page 44, put your pencils down. You may now begin.**

Allow students time to find and mark their answers.

7 Katya has started a coin collection. She has 12 coins worth at least $2 each. Two of the coins are worth $4 each. **How can Katya figure out how much the 12 coins are worth?**

A Multiply 12 times 2, and add this amount to 2 times 4.

B Multiply 10 times 2, and add this amount to 2 times 4.

C Multiply 12 times 2, and add this amount to $4.

D Multiply 12 times 2.

8 One fourth of the science class did extra-credit reports. There were 6 extra-credit reports. **How many students are in the science class?**

J 6   **L** 24

K 18   **M** 28

9 Luis planned to buy a new shirt. The store had red, white, and blue shirts that he liked. Each color was available with or without a pocket. **How many different combinations did Luis have to choose from?**

A 3   **C** 6

B 5   **D** 18

10 Talia bought a bolt of ribbon 8 yards long for a craft project. **How can she figure how many $\frac{1}{4}$-yard pieces she can cut from the 8 yards?**

J Multiply 8 by $\frac{1}{4}$

K Divide 8 by $\frac{1}{4}$

L Add 8 and $\frac{1}{4}$

M Subtract $\frac{1}{4}$ from 8

11 Lauren packed 58 muffins into boxes of 12 each. **How many muffins will be left over?**

A 2   **C** 8

B 4   **D** 10

Use the graph below to answer questions 12–14.

Monthly Bike Sales

12 **Which month shows the fewest sales?**

J January

K September

L November

M December

13 **About how many more bikes were sold in April than in November?**

A 5   **C** 5

B 10   **D** 25

14 **Which best describes sales between March and June?**

J Bike sales increased steadily.

K Bike sales fell steadily each month.

L Bike sales rose sharply then fell.

M Bike sales fell slightly then rose sharply.

GO ON

Level 12

Use the graph below to answer questions 15–17.

Sources of Income during June

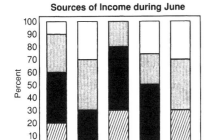

- ☐ chores
- ■ allowance
- ▨ paper route
- ▨ baby-sitting

15 Which person did not receive an allowance?

A Betsy

B Carol

C Dan

D Erwin

16 How did Carol make most of her money?

J From chores

K From a paper route

L From allowance

M From baby-sitting

17 What percent of his income did Al receive from a paper route?

A 10%

B 20%

C 30%

D 40%

Use the graph below to answer questions 18–20.

Swim Classes Offered

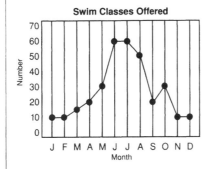

18 How many more classes were offered in June than in December?

J 10

K 50

L 60

M 70

19 During which season were the most swim classes offered?

A Spring

B Summer

C Fall

D Winter

20 Which best describes the number of swim classes offered between January and July?

J The number changed little.

K The number fell sharply.

L The number rose sharply after May.

M The number rose after a slight fall.

STOP

Level 12

Answers

44

15 Ⓐ Ⓑ Ⓒ ●   17 Ⓐ ● Ⓒ Ⓓ   19 Ⓐ ● Ⓒ Ⓓ

16 Ⓙ Ⓚ ● Ⓜ   18 ● Ⓙ Ⓛ Ⓜ   20 Ⓙ Ⓚ ● Ⓜ

SAY: **It is now time to stop. You have completed the Unit 7 Test. Make sure that you have carefully filled in your answer spaces and have completely erased any stray marks. Then put your pencils down.**

After the test has been scored, review the questions and answer choices with students. If students are having difficulty with any lesson, provide them with additional practice items.

―――― **Lesson 18: Adding** ――――

Directions: Darken the circle for the correct answer. Darken the circle for **N** if the answer is <u>not</u> given.

| TRY THIS | First, check the fractions. If necessary, change the fractions so that the denominators are the same. Next, add the numerators. Finally, reduce the fraction answer to lowest terms, if possible. |

S1 $\frac{1}{3} + \frac{1}{6} =$

A $\frac{2}{9}$
B $\frac{2}{6}$
C $\frac{1}{2}$
D N

| THINK IT THROUGH | The correct answer is C. First, rename $\frac{1}{3}$ as $\frac{2}{6}$. Next, add the fractions $\frac{2}{6}$ and $\frac{1}{6}$ to get $\frac{3}{6}$. Last, reduce $\frac{3}{6}$ to $\frac{1}{2}$. |

STOP

―――――――――――

Reduce answers that are fractions to lowest terms.

1
$\frac{3}{8}$
$+\frac{1}{4}$

A $\frac{1}{3}$
B $\frac{1}{2}$
C $\frac{5}{8}$
D N

4   $0.4 + 0.5 =$

J 0.09
K 0.9
L 9.0
M N

2
$\frac{3}{20} + \frac{7}{20} + \frac{9}{20} =$

J $\frac{1}{2}$
K $\frac{19}{20}$
L $\frac{19}{60}$
M N

5
8.3
5.6
14.1
$+ 11.0$

A 29.0
B 38.0
C 39.0
D N

3   $4527 + 3664 =$

A 7181
B 8191
C 8201
D N

6   $0.0402 + 0.203 =$

J 0.602
K 0.2432
L 2.432
M N

STOP

Level 12

Answers
S1 Ⓐ Ⓑ ● Ⓓ   2 Ⓙ ● Ⓛ Ⓜ   4 Ⓙ ● Ⓛ Ⓜ   6 Ⓙ ● Ⓛ Ⓜ
1 Ⓐ Ⓑ ● Ⓓ   3 Ⓐ ● Ⓒ Ⓓ   5 Ⓐ Ⓑ ● Ⓓ

45

UNIT 8 Math Computation

Lesson 18: Adding

Mathematics Skills: Horizontal and vertical addition of whole numbers, decimals, fractions, and mixed numbers

Distribute scratch paper to students. Tell them to compute their answers on the scratch paper.

SAY: **Turn to Lesson 18, Adding, on page 45.**

Check to see that all students find Lesson 18.

SAY: **In Lesson 18 you will practice adding whole numbers, decimals, fractions, and mixed numbers.**

Read the <u>Directions</u> to students.

SAY: **Now look at <u>Try This</u>.**

Read <u>Try This</u> to students.

SAY: **Now look at S1. You are asked to add $\frac{1}{3}$ and $\frac{1}{6}$. Work the problem, then darken the circle for the correct answer. If the correct answer is not given, darken the circle for <u>N</u>.**

Allow students time to find and mark their answer.

SAY: **Now look at <u>Think It Through</u>.**

Read <u>Think It Through</u> to students. Check to see that all students have filled in the correct answer space. Remind students to reduce answers that are fractions to lowest terms. Ask students if they have any questions.

SAY: **Now you will practice solving more addition problems. Do numbers 1 through 6 just as we did S1. When you come to the word *STOP* at the bottom of page 45, put your pencils down. You may now begin.**

Allow students time to find and mark their answers.

Review the questions and answer choices with students. Discuss with the class why one answer is correct and the others are not correct. Also check to see that students have carefully filled in the answer spaces and have completely erased any stray marks.

Directions: Darken the circle for the correct answer. Darken the circle for N if the answer is not given.

TRY THIS Remember to regroup when necessary. Check your answer by covering the top number and adding the answer and the second number. The covered number and the sum should be equal.

S1

A 784
B 785
C 816
D N

THINK IT THROUGH The correct answer is A. It is necessary to regroup the 800 as 7 hundreds, 9 tens, and 10 ones. Check the answer by adding 16 and 784.

STOP

Reduce answers that are fractions to lowest terms.

1

A $\frac{1}{3}$
B $\frac{5}{12}$
C $\frac{5}{6}$
D N

5

A $\frac{3}{10}$
B $\frac{1}{2}$
C $\frac{5}{5}$
D N

2 $6.3 - 4.6 =$

J 0.17
K 1.7
L 10.9
M N

6

J $\frac{1}{6}$
K $\frac{1}{3}$
L $1\frac{1}{2}$
M N

3

A $\frac{3}{8}$
B $\frac{3}{4}$
C $1\frac{1}{2}$
D N

7 $0.316 - 0.307 =$

A 0.009
B 0.623
C 0.9
D N

4

J 346
K 356
L 480
M N

8

J 338
K 348
L 438
M N

STOP

Level 12

Answers

46

S1 ● Ⓑ Ⓒ Ⓓ   2 Ⓙ ● Ⓛ Ⓜ   4 ● Ⓚ Ⓛ Ⓜ   6 Ⓙ ● Ⓛ Ⓜ   8 ● Ⓚ Ⓛ Ⓜ
1 ● Ⓑ Ⓒ Ⓓ   3 Ⓐ ● Ⓒ Ⓓ   5 ● Ⓑ Ⓒ Ⓓ   7 ● Ⓑ Ⓒ Ⓓ

Lesson 19: Subtracting

Mathematics Skills: Horizontal and vertical subtraction of whole numbers, decimals, fractions, and mixed numbers

Distribute scratch paper to students. Tell them to compute their answers on the scratch paper.

SAY: **Turn to Lesson 19, Subtracting, on page 46.**

Check to see that all students find Lesson 19.

SAY: **In Lesson 19 you will practice subtracting whole numbers, decimals, fractions, and mixed numbers.**

Read the Directions to students.

SAY: **Now look at Try This.**

Read Try This to students.

SAY: **Now look at S1. You are asked to subtract 16 from 800. Work the problem, then darken the circle for the correct answer. If the correct answer is not given, darken the circle for N.**

Allow students time to find and mark their answer.

SAY: **Now look at Think It Through.**

Read Think It Through to students. Check to see that all students have filled in the correct answer space. Remind students to reduce answers that are fractions to lowest terms. Ask students if they have any questions.

SAY: **Now you will practice solving more subtraction problems. Do numbers 1 through 8 just as we did S1. When you come to the word *STOP* at the bottom of page 46, put your pencils down. You may now begin.**

Allow students time to find and mark their answers.

Review the questions and answer choices with students. Discuss with the class why one answer is correct and the others are not correct. Also check to see that students have carefully filled in the answer spaces and have completely erased any stray marks.

Lesson 20: Multiplying

Directions: Darken the circle for the correct answer. Darken the circle for <u>N</u> if the answer is <u>not</u> given.

 TRY THIS — Remember to write a zero in the ones place as a place holder when you multiply by a two-digit number.

S1

508
× 63

A 32,000
B 32,040
C 32,400
D N

THINK IT THROUGH — The correct answer is D. First, multiply by the ones place. Next, write a zero in the ones place as a place holder and multiply by the tens place. Last, add the two numbers together.

STOP

1

54 × 70 =

A 780
B 3780
C 37800
D N

2

5000 × 80 =

J 40,000
K 400,000
L 4,000,000
M N

3

0.17
× 0.03

A 0.0051
B 0.2
C 0.51
D N

4

 $\frac{1}{8} \times \frac{1}{2} =$

J $\frac{1}{16}$
K $\frac{1}{6}$
L $\frac{1}{4}$
M N

5

0.32 × 0.3 =

A 0.096
B 0.96
C 9.6
D N

6

0.34
× 5

J 0.17
K 1.7
L 17
M N

7

648 × 33 =

A 3888
B 20,384
C 21,384
D N

8

$\frac{1}{4}$
× 8

J $\frac{1}{2}$
K 2
L $8\frac{1}{4}$
M N

STOP

Level 12

Answers

S1 Ⓐ Ⓑ Ⓒ ●   2 Ⓙ ● Ⓛ Ⓜ   4 ● Ⓚ Ⓛ Ⓜ   6 Ⓙ ● Ⓛ Ⓜ   8 Ⓙ ● Ⓛ Ⓜ
1 Ⓐ ● Ⓒ Ⓓ   3 ● Ⓑ Ⓒ Ⓓ   5 ● Ⓑ Ⓒ Ⓓ   7 Ⓐ Ⓑ ● Ⓓ

47

Lesson 20: Multiplying

Mathematics Skills: Horizontal and vertical multiplication of whole numbers, fractions, and decimals

Distribute scratch paper to students. Tell them to compute their answers on the scratch paper.

SAY: **Turn to Lesson 20, Multiplying, on page 47.**

Check to see that all students find Lesson 20.

SAY: **In Lesson 20 you will practice multiplying whole numbers, fractions, and decimals.**

Read the <u>Directions</u> to students.

SAY: **Now look at <u>Try This.</u>**

Read <u>Try This</u> to students.

SAY: **Now look at S1. You are asked to multiply 508 by 63. Work the problem, then darken the circle for the correct answer. If the correct answer is not given, darken the circle for <u>N</u>.**

Allow students time to find and mark their answer.

SAY: **Now look at <u>Think It Through.</u>**

Read <u>Think It Through</u> to students. Check to see that all students have filled in the correct answer space. Remind students to reduce answers that are fractions to lowest terms. Ask students if they have any questions.

SAY: **Now you will practice solving more multiplication problems. Do numbers 1 through 8 just as we did S1. When you come to the word *STOP* at the bottom of page 47, put your pencils down. You may now begin.**

Allow students time to find and mark their answers.

Review the questions and answer choices with students. Discuss with the class why one answer is correct and the others are not correct. Also check to see that students have carefully filled in the answer spaces and have completely erased any stray marks.

Lesson 21: Dividing

Directions: Darken the circle for the correct answer. Darken the circle for <u>N</u> if the answer is <u>not</u> given.

> **TRY THIS**
>
> Check the answer to a division problem by multiplying the answer by the divisor in the problem. Then add any remainder. The result should equal the dividend.

S1

A 150 r2
B 152
C 152 r2
D N

> **THINK IT THROUGH**
>
> The correct answer is C. Check this by multiplying 152 by 4 to get 608. Then, add the remainder 2 to get 610.

STOP

1

A 81 r6
B 83
C 656
D N

2 24)975

J 4 r15
K 39
L 41
M N

3 7)133

A 10 r5
B 18 r5
C 19
D N

4 7)4438

J 633
K 634
L 734
M N

5 88 ÷ 10 =

A 0.88
B 8.8
C 8
D N

6 848 ÷ 36 =

J 20
K 20 r28
L 23 r20
M N

7 4208 ÷ 8 =

A 56
B 526
C 530
D N

8 57 ÷ 10 =

J 0.57
K 5.7
L 570
M N

STOP

Level 12

Answers
S1 Ⓐ Ⓑ ● Ⓓ   2 Ⓙ Ⓚ Ⓛ ●   4 Ⓙ ● Ⓛ Ⓜ   6 Ⓙ Ⓚ ● Ⓜ   8 Ⓙ ● Ⓛ Ⓜ
48   1 Ⓐ ● Ⓒ Ⓓ   3 Ⓐ Ⓑ ● Ⓓ   5 Ⓐ ● Ⓒ Ⓓ   7 Ⓐ ● Ⓒ Ⓓ

Lesson 21: Dividing

Mathematics Skill: Division of whole numbers

Distribute scratch paper to students. Tell them to compute their answers on the scratch paper.

SAY: **Turn to Lesson 21, Dividing, on page 48.**

Check to see that all students find Lesson 21.

SAY: **In Lesson 21 you will practice dividing whole numbers.**

Read the Directions to students.

SAY: **Now look at Try This.**

Read Try This to students.

SAY: **Now look at S1. You are asked to divide 610 by 4. Work the problem, then darken the circle for the correct answer. If the correct answer is not given, darken the circle for <u>N</u>.**

Allow students time to find and mark their answer.

SAY: **Now look at Think It Through.**

Read Think It Through to students. Check to see that all students have filled in the correct answer space. Ask students if they have any questions.

SAY: **Now you will practice solving more division problems. Do numbers 1 through 8 just as we did S1. When you come to the word _STOP_ at the bottom of page 48, put your pencils down. You may now begin.**

Allow students time to find and mark their answers.

Review the questions and answer choices with students. Discuss with the class why one answer is correct and the others are not correct. Also check to see that students have carefully filled in the answer spaces and have completely erased any stray marks.

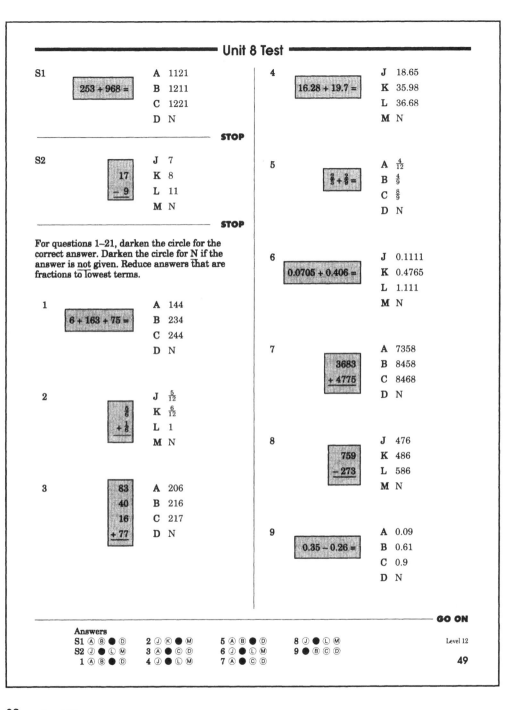

Unit 8 Test

S1 $253 + 968 =$
- A 1121
- B 1211
- C 1221
- D N

STOP

S2 $17 - 9$
- J 7
- K 8
- L 11
- M N

STOP

For questions 1–21, darken the circle for the correct answer. Darken the circle for N if the answer is not given. Reduce answers that are fractions to lowest terms.

1 $6 + 163 + 75 =$
- A 144
- B 234
- C 244
- D N

2 $\frac{5}{6} + \frac{1}{6}$
- J $\frac{5}{12}$
- K $\frac{6}{12}$
- L 1
- M N

3 $83 + 40 + 16 + 77$
- A 206
- B 216
- C 217
- D N

4 $16.28 + 19.7 =$
- J 18.65
- K 35.98
- L 36.68
- M N

5 $\frac{2}{3} + \frac{2}{3} =$
- A $\frac{4}{12}$
- B $\frac{4}{9}$
- C $\frac{8}{9}$
- D N

6 $0.0705 + 0.406 =$
- J 0.1111
- K 0.4765
- L 1.111
- M N

7 $3683 + 4775$
- A 7358
- B 8458
- C 8468
- D N

8 $759 - 273$
- J 476
- K 486
- L 586
- M N

9 $0.35 - 0.26 =$
- A 0.09
- B 0.61
- C 0.9
- D N

GO ON

Answers
S1 Ⓐ Ⓑ ● Ⓓ
S2 Ⓙ ● Ⓛ Ⓜ
1 Ⓐ Ⓑ ● Ⓓ
2 Ⓙ Ⓚ ● Ⓜ
3 Ⓐ ● Ⓒ Ⓓ
4 Ⓙ Ⓚ ● Ⓜ
5 Ⓐ Ⓑ ● Ⓓ
6 Ⓙ ● Ⓛ Ⓜ
7 Ⓐ ● Ⓒ Ⓓ
8 Ⓙ ● Ⓛ Ⓜ
9 ● Ⓑ Ⓒ Ⓓ

Level 12

49

Unit 8 Test

Distribute scratch paper to students. Tell them to compute their answers on the scratch paper.

SAY: **Turn to the Unit 8 Test on page 49.**

Check to see that all students find the Unit 8 Test.

SAY: **In this test you will use the mathematics skills that we have practiced in this unit. Look at S1. You are asked to add 253 and 968. Darken the circle for the correct answer. If the correct answer is not given, darken the circle for N.**

Allow students time to find and mark their answer.

SAY: **You should have darkened the circle for *C* because *253 + 968 = 1221*.**

Check to see that all students have filled in the correct answer space. Ask students if they have any questions.

SAY: **Now look at S2. You are asked to subtract 9 from 17. Darken the circle for the correct answer. If the correct answer is not given, darken the circle for N.**

Allow students time to find and mark their answer.

SAY: **You should have darkened the circle for *K* because *17 – 9 = 8*.**

Check to see that all students have filled in the correct answer space. Ask students if they have any questions.

SAY: **Now you will finish the test on your own. Do numbers 1 through 21 just as we did the samples. Read the problems and answer choices carefully. Then darken the circle for each correct answer. If the correct answer is not given, darken the circle for N. When you come to the words *GO ON* at the bottom of a page, continue working on the next page. When you come to the word *STOP* at the bottom of page 50, put your pencils down. You may now begin.**

Allow students time to find and mark their answers.

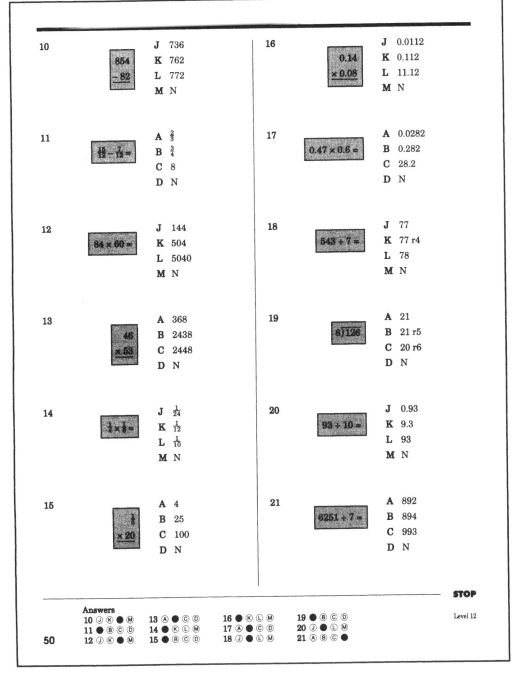

10　
854
− 82

J 736
K 762
L 772
M N

11　$\frac{11}{12} - \frac{7}{12} =$

A $\frac{2}{3}$
B $\frac{3}{4}$
C 8
D N

12　$84 \times 60 =$

J 144
K 504
L 5040
M N

13　
46
× 53

A 368
B 2438
C 2448
D N

14　$\frac{1}{4} \times \frac{1}{6} =$

J $\frac{1}{24}$
K $\frac{1}{12}$
L $\frac{1}{10}$
M N

15　
$\frac{1}{5}$
× 20

A 4
B 25
C 100
D N

16　
0.14
× 0.08

J 0.0112
K 0.112
L 11.12
M N

17　$0.47 \times 0.6 =$

A 0.0282
B 0.282
C 28.2
D N

18　$543 \div 7 =$

J 77
K 77 r4
L 78
M N

19　$6 \overline{)126}$

A 21
B 21 r5
C 20 r6
D N

20　$93 \div 10 =$

J 0.93
K 9.3
L 93
M N

21　$6251 \div 7 =$

A 892
B 894
C 993
D N

STOP

Answers

10 Ⓙ Ⓚ ● Ⓜ   13 Ⓐ ● Ⓒ Ⓓ   16 ● Ⓚ Ⓛ Ⓜ   19 ● Ⓑ Ⓒ Ⓓ
11 ● Ⓑ Ⓒ Ⓓ   14 ● Ⓚ Ⓛ Ⓜ   17 Ⓐ ● Ⓒ Ⓓ   20 Ⓙ ● Ⓛ Ⓜ
50
12 Ⓙ Ⓚ ● Ⓜ   15 ● Ⓑ Ⓒ Ⓓ   18 Ⓙ ● Ⓛ Ⓜ   21 Ⓐ Ⓑ Ⓒ ●

Level 12

SAY: **It is now time to stop. You have completed the Unit 8 Test. Make sure that you have carefully filled in your answer spaces and have completely erased any stray marks. Then put your pencils down.**

After the test has been scored, review the questions and answer choices with students. If students are having difficulty, provide them with additional practice.

UNIT 9 Maps and Diagrams

Lesson 22: Working with Maps

Directions: Darken the circle for the correct answer.

| TRY THIS | Study the map key. It tells you what the symbols on the map mean. A compass rose shows direction. A distance scale is used to find the distance on a map. |

S1

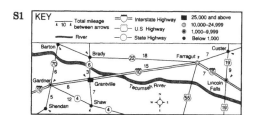

Which highway passes through Grantville and Lincoln Falls?

A ⑩
B ㉒
C ㊌
D ⑦⓪

| THINK IT THROUGH | The correct answer is **A**. Interstate Highway 10 runs northwestward, passes through Grantville, turns southeastward at Farragut, and then passes through Lincoln Falls. |

STOP

Use the map in S1 to answer questions 1–5.

1 Which might be the population of Lincoln Falls?

A 376   C 13,402
B 7,896   D 31,227

2 Walt is planning to drive from Sheridan to Barton on State Highway 70. **How many miles will he have left to drive when he reaches Gardner?**

J 5 miles   L 8 miles
K 6 miles   M 11 miles

3 Which highways do not cross the Tecumseh River?

A ㊌ and ⑦⓪   C ④ and ㉒
B ⑩ and ⑲   D ⑥ and ⑩

4 What is the mileage between Shaw and Farragut by the shortest route, using only state highways?

J 28 miles
K 25 miles
L 22 miles
M 10 miles

5 Which city is located 10 miles north and 25 miles east of Shaw?

A Lincoln Falls
B Custer
C Farragut
D Brady

GO ON

Level 12

Answers
S1 ●ⒷⒸⒹ   2 Ⓙ●ⓁⓂ   4 ●ⓀⓁⓂ
1 Ⓐ●ⒸⒹ   3 ⒶⒷ●Ⓓ   5 Ⓐ●ⒸⒹ

51

UNIT 9 Maps and Diagrams

Lesson 22: Working with Maps

Study Skills: Using map symbols and keys to describe and locate places; determining direction and distance; interpreting data on population, transportation, elevation, and resources; tracing travel routes

SAY: **Turn to Lesson 22, Working with Maps, page 51.**

Check to see that all students find Lesson 22.

SAY: **In Lesson 22 you will practice using maps to answer questions.**

Read the <u>Directions</u> to students.

SAY: **Now look at <u>Try This</u>.**

Read <u>Try This</u> to students.

SAY: **Now look at S1. Study the map and key to see what the symbols mean and where they are located. Study the compass rose to find directions. (Allow one minute for students to study the map.) Now read the question and answer choices carefully. Then darken the circle for the choice that shows which highway passes through Lincoln Falls and Gardner.**

Allow students time to find and mark their answer.

SAY: **Now look at <u>Think It Through</u>.**

Read <u>Think It Through</u> to students. Check to see that students have filled in the correct answer space. Ask students if they have any questions.

SAY: **Now you will practice using maps to answer more questions. Do numbers 1 through 10 just as we did S1. When you come to the words *GO ON* at the bottom of a page, continue working on the next page. When you come to the word *STOP* at the bottom of page 52, put your pencils down. You may now begin.**

Allow students time to find and mark their answers.

The maps below show an imaginary country made up of four states. The top map shows major cities, bodies of water, and main railroads. The bottom map shows resources of the country. Use these maps to answer questions 6–10.

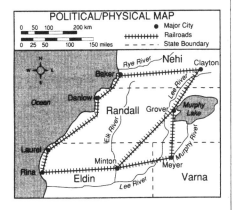

POLITICAL/PHYSICAL MAP

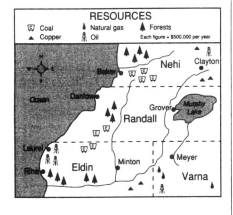

RESOURCES

6 About how many miles by railroad is the shortest route from Baker to Grover?

J   100 miles

K   150 miles

L   250 miles

M   400 miles

7 Where is natural gas found in this country?

A   Eldin

B   Varna

C   Nehi

D   Randall

8 In which city might oil refining be an important industry?

J   Baker

K   Minton

L   Grover

M   Laurel

9 What is the value of forests in Nehi each year?

A $2,500,000

B $2,000,000

C $1,500,000

D $500,000

10 Which resource is most likely shipped out of Baker by railroad?

J   Oil

K   Coal

L   Natural gas

M   Copper

STOP

Level 12

Answers

6 Ⓙ Ⓚ ● Ⓜ   8 Ⓙ Ⓚ Ⓛ ●   10 Ⓙ ● Ⓛ Ⓜ

52   7 Ⓐ ● Ⓒ Ⓓ   9 Ⓐ ● Ⓒ Ⓓ

Lesson 23: Working with Charts and Diagrams

Directions: Darken the circle for the correct answer.

TRY THIS | Before you select your answer, carefully read all the information given in the diagram.

S1

RIVEREDGE SOFTBALL TOURNAMENT

Jets — Bob's
Bob's Bombers — Bombers — Andy's
Andy's Arrows — Andy's — Arrows
Rockford Rockets — Arrows — Northern
Springville Tigers — Northern — Legends
Northern Legends — Legends — Northern
White Lightning — Rolling — Legends
Rolling Thunder — Thunder

How many teams played in the first round of the softball tournament?

A 1   C 4
B 2   D 8

THINK IT THROUGH | The correct answer is D. The far left part of the diagram names the eight teams that played in the first round of the tournament.

STOP

Use the diagram in S1 to answer questions 1–4.

1 Which team won the softball tournament?
   A Jets
   B Northern Legends
   C Andy's Arrows
   D Rolling Thunder

2 Which four teams won their first game in the tournament?
   J Jets, Rockford Rockets, Springville Tigers, White Lightning
   K Jets, Andy's Arrows, Springville Tigers, Rolling Thunder
   L Bob's Bombers, Andy's Arrows, Northern Legends, Rolling Thunder
   M Jets, Rockford Rockets, Northern Legends, White Lightning

3 Which team placed second in the tournament?
   A Northern Legends
   B Rolling Thunder
   C Andy's Arrows
   D Springville Tigers

4 Which teams could have eliminated the second place team during the first round of the tournament, before the championship game?
   J Jets and Andy's Arrows
   K Rockford Rockets and Bob's Bombers
   L Northern Legends and Springville Tigers
   M White Lightning and Rolling Thunder

GO ON

Answers
S1 Ⓐ Ⓑ Ⓒ ●   2 Ⓙ Ⓚ ● Ⓜ   4 Ⓙ ● Ⓛ Ⓜ
1 Ⓐ ● Ⓒ Ⓓ   3 Ⓐ Ⓑ ● Ⓓ

Level 12

53

Lesson 23: Working with Charts and Diagrams

Study Skills: Interpreting information in schedules, charts, tables, and diagrams

SAY: **Turn to Lesson 23, Working with Charts and Diagrams, page 53.**

Check to see that all students find Lesson 23.

SAY: **In Lesson 23 you will practice interpreting information presented in visual materials.**

Read the Directions to students.

SAY: **Now look at Try This.**

Read Try This to students.

SAY: **Now look at S1. Study the diagram. Read the question and answer choices carefully. Then darken the circle for the choice that shows how many teams played in the first round of the softball tournament.**

Allow students time to find and mark their answer.

SAY: **Now look at Think It Through.**

Read Think It Through to students. Check to see that students have filled in the correct answer space. Ask students if they have any questions.

SAY: **Now you will practice interpreting information presented in other visual materials to answer more questions. Do numbers 1 through 10 just as we did S1. When you come to the words *GO ON* at the bottom of a page, continue working on the next page. When you come to the word *STOP* at the bottom of page 54, put your pencils down. You may now begin.**

Allow students time to find and mark their answers.

Use the table shown here to answer questions 5–7.

FLIGHTS FROM ST. CLARE				
Destination	Departure	Arrival	Airline & Flight #	Meal
Piedmont	5:15 a.m. 2:20 p.m.	7:49 a.m. 5:05 p.m.	UA 12 UA 339	Breakfast Snack
Charleston	10:30 a.m.	11:10 a.m.	AC 99	—
Cameron	5:15 p.m.	6:05 p.m.	SS 503	Snack
King City	12:45 p.m. 7:30 p.m.	4:15 p.m. 10:30 p.m.	WF 157 GA 291	Lunch Dinner
Douglas	6:00 a.m. 4:50 p.m.	9:30 a.m. 6:25 p.m.	UA 199 AC 201	Breakfast Dinner
Milledgeville	7:30 p.m. 8:15 p.m.	9:50 p.m. 10:35 p.m.	SS 103 SS 84	Dinner Snack
Columbia	10:45 a.m.	11:56 a.m.	UA 57	—

AC—Air Clipper   UA—Urban Air
GA—Global Airlines   WF—World Fliers
SS—Southeast Skies

5 **Which flight takes fewer than two hours?**

A GA 291

B WF 157

C SS 84

D AC 99

6 **Which airline offers early morning departures to Piedmont and Douglas?**

J Urban Air

K World Fliers

L Air Clipper

M Global Airlines

7 **If you left St. Clare at 5:15 P.M., what time would you arrive in Cameron?**

A 6:25 P.M.

B 6:05 P.M.

C 10:35 P.M.

D 11:10 P.M.

Use the chart shown here to answer questions 8–10.

COLONIAL COLLEGES		
Date Founded	Original Name	Name Today
1636	Harvard College	Same
1693	College of William and Mary of Virginia	College of William and Mary
1701	Yale College	Same
1746	College of New Jersey	Princeton University
1751	Philadelphia Academy	University of Pennsylvania
1754	King's College	Columbia University
1764	Rhode Island College	Brown University
1766	Queen's College	Rutgers University
1769	Dartmouth College	Same

8 **Which college is located in Rhode Island?**

J College of William and Mary

K Philadelphia Academy

L Princeton University

M Brown University

9 **What is the oldest college listed in the chart?**

A Dartmouth College

B Columbia University

C Harvard University

D Brown University

10 **How is the information in this chart arranged?**

J alphabetically by the name of the college today

K by size

L chronologically by the date founded

M alphabetically by the original name of the college

STOP

Level 12

Answers

54

5 Ⓐ Ⓑ Ⓒ ●   7 Ⓐ ● Ⓒ Ⓓ   9 Ⓐ Ⓑ ● Ⓓ

6 ● Ⓚ Ⓛ Ⓜ   8 Ⓙ Ⓚ Ⓛ ●   10 Ⓙ Ⓚ ● Ⓜ

Unit 9 Test

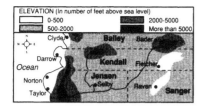

S1

ELEVATION (In number of feet above sea level)

☐ 0-500	▨ 2000-5000
▨ 500-2000	■ More than 5000

Clyde · Bailey · Bader · *Ocean* · Darrow · Kendall · Fletcher · Norton · Jensen · Selby · Raven · Taylor · Sanger

Which city has the highest elevation?

A Selby

B Bader

C Taylor

D Fletcher

STOP

For questions 1–10, darken the circle for the correct answer.

The maps below show an imaginary country made of up four states. Use the maps to answer questions 1–5.

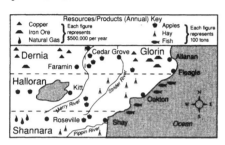

Resources/Products (Annual) Key

▲ Copper ▲ Iron Ore ▲ Natural Gas — Each figure represents $500,000 per year

🍎 Apples 🌾 Hay 🐟 Fish — Each figure represents 100 tons

Dernia · Faramin · Cedar Grove · Glorin · Allanan · Fleagle · Halloran · Kitt · *Strider River* · Oakton · *Merry River* · Roseville · Shay · *Ocean* · Shannara · *Pippin River*

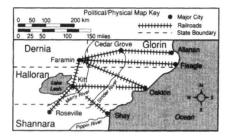

Political/Physical Map Key

0 50 100 200 km

0 25 50 150 miles

● Major City · ┼┼┼┼ Railroads · – – – State Boundary

Dernia · Faramin · Cedar Grove · Glorin · Allanan · Fleagle · Halloran · Lake Leah · Kitt · *Merry River* · *Strider River* · Oakton · Roseville · Shay · *Ocean* · Shannara · *Pippin River*

1 What is the value of the iron ore produced in Dernia each year?

A $2,000,000

B $1,500,000

C $1,000,000

D $500,000

2 What is the shortest distance by railroad between Faramin and Oakton?

J 150 miles

K 325 miles

L 400 miles

M 375 miles

3 Which city probably uses transportation by water as well as by railroad?

A Roseville

B Cedar Grove

C Kitt

D Fleagle

4 In which state is fishing an important part of the economy?

J Dernia

K Glorin

L Halloran

M Shannara

5 Which product is most likely shipped out of Faramin by railroad?

A Copper

B Fish

C Natural gas

D Iron ore

GO ON

Level 12

Answers

S1 Ⓐ ● Ⓒ Ⓓ

1 Ⓐ Ⓑ Ⓒ ●

2 ● Ⓚ Ⓛ Ⓜ

3 Ⓐ Ⓑ Ⓒ ●

4 Ⓙ Ⓚ ● Ⓜ

5 ● Ⓑ Ⓒ Ⓓ

55

Unit 9 Test

SAY: **Turn to the Unit 9 Test on page 55.**

Check to see that all students find the Unit 9 Test.

SAY: **In this test you will use the study skills that we have practiced in this unit. Look at S1. Study the map and key. You are asked to tell which city has the highest elevation. Darken the circle for the correct answer.**

Allow students time to find and mark their answer.

SAY: **You should have darkened the circle for *B* because *Bader* has the highest elevation.**

Check to see that all students have filled in the correct answer space. Ask students if they have any questions.

SAY: **Now you will finish the test on your own. Do numbers 1 through 10 just as we did S1. Study the visual materials. Read the questions and answer choices carefully. Then darken the circle for each correct answer. When you come to the words *GO ON* at the bottom of a page, continue working on the next page. When you come to the word *STOP* at the bottom of page 56, put your pencils down. You may now begin.**

Allow students time to find and mark their answers.

Use the following diagram to answer questions 6 and 7.

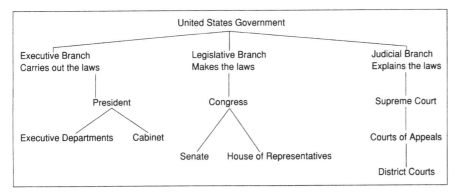

6 **What court heads the judicial branch of the United States government?**

J District Courts

K Congress

L Courts of Appeals

M Supreme Court

7 **Into what two parts is the legislative branch of the United States government divided?**

A Supreme Court and Courts of Appeals

B Executive departments and Cabinet

C Senate and House of Representatives

D President and Supreme Court

Use the following table to answer questions 8–10.

NAMES OF ANIMALS AND THEIR YOUNG

Animal	Male	Female	Young	Group
Bear	boar	sow	cub	sloth
Deer	stag	doe	fawn	herd
Fox	dog	vixen	cub	skulk
Seal	bull	cow	pup	herd
Swan	cob	pen	cygnet	flock
Whale	bull	cow	calf	herd

8 **What is a male swan called?**

J dog   L vixen

K cob   M skulk

9 **Which animals form groups called herds?**

A bears and swans

B swans and whales

C deer, foxes, and seals

D deer, seals, and whales

10 **How is the information in this table arranged?**

J by number of animal young

K alphabetically by animal

L by size of animal

M alphabetically by group

STOP

Level 12

Answers

56

6 Ⓙ Ⓚ Ⓛ ●   8 Ⓙ ● Ⓛ Ⓜ   10 Ⓙ ● Ⓛ Ⓜ

7 Ⓐ Ⓑ ● Ⓓ   9 Ⓐ Ⓑ Ⓒ ●

SAY: **It is now time to stop. You have completed the Unit 9 Test. Make sure that you have carefully filled in your answer spaces and have completely erased any stray marks. Then put your pencils down.**

After the test has been scored, review the questions and answer choices with students. If students are having difficulty, provide them with additional practice.

UNIT 10 Reference Materials

Lesson 24: Using an Index

Lesson 24: Using an Index

Directions: Study the index below, and read each question carefully. Then darken the circle for the correct answer.

TRY THIS Remember that an index is an alphabetical list of a book's subjects. It gives the page numbers where the subjects can be found.

S1 On which page does an explanation of how to care for a camera begin?

A 20
B 52
C 141
D 216

THINK IT THROUGH The correct answer is A. According to the index, information on the care and cleaning of a camera begins on page 20 and continues through page 28.

STOP

INDEX

Action photography, news, 130;
 sports, 136–140
Animals, in nature, 193–198; portraits, 216

Black-and-white photography, filters, 86;
 types of film, 18–19

Camera, care and cleaning, 20–28;
 history, 1–10;
Color photography, filters, 141; film, 14–15

Fashion photography, adults, 113;
 children, 117
Filters, blue, 52–53; green, 98–99;
 yellow, 92–93

Lenses, care, cleaning, 28; telephoto, 60;
 wide angle, 58; zoom, 63

1 Which page would have information about photographing wild animals?

A 1
B 130
C 193
D 216

2 Which page might provide information about using a yellow filter to improve outdoor photography?

J 52
K 92
L 98
M 130

3 Which page might describe how to clean sand from a telephoto lens?

A 19
B 28
C 58
D 63

4 Which page describes the kinds of filters used in color photography?

J 14
K 18
L 86
M 141

5 Which page might discuss how early cameras differed from modern ones?

A 10
B 28
C 99
D 117

STOP

Answers
S1 ● Ⓑ Ⓒ Ⓓ   2 Ⓙ ● Ⓛ Ⓜ   4 Ⓙ Ⓚ Ⓛ ●
1 Ⓐ Ⓑ ● Ⓓ   3 Ⓐ ● Ⓒ Ⓓ   5 ● Ⓑ Ⓒ Ⓓ

Level 12

57

Study Skill: Using an index to locate information

SAY: **Turn to Lesson 24, Using an Index, on page 57.**

Check to see that all students find Lesson 24.

SAY: **In Lesson 24 you will practice using an index to learn where information is located in a book.**

Read the Directions to students.

SAY: **Now look at Try This.**

Read Try This to students.

SAY: **Now look at S1. Study the sample index. Read the question and answer choices carefully. Then darken the circle for the first page on which you would find an explanation of how to care for a camera.**

Allow students time to find and mark their answer.

SAY: **Now look at Think It Through.**

Read Think It Through to students. Check to see that students have filled in the correct answer space. Ask students if they have any questions.

SAY: **Now you will use the sample index to answer more questions. Do numbers 1 through 5 just as we did S1. When you come to the word *STOP* at the bottom of page 57, put your pencils down. You may now begin.**

Allow students time to find and mark their answers.

UNIT 10 Reference Materials

Lesson 24: Using an Index

Directions: Study the index below, and read each question carefully. Then darken the circle for the correct answer.

TRY THIS — Remember that an index is an alphabetical list of a book's subjects. It gives the page numbers where the subjects can be found.

S1 On which page does an explanation of how to care for a camera begin?

A 20   C 141

B 52   D 216

THINK IT THROUGH — The correct answer is A. According to the index, information on the care and cleaning of a camera begins on page 20 and continues through page 28.

STOP

INDEX

Action photography, news, 130;
  sports, 136–140
Animals, in nature, 193–198; portraits, 216

Black-and-white photography, filters, 86;
  types of film, 18–19

Camera, care and cleaning, 20–28;
  history, 1–10;
Color photography, filters, 141; film, 14–15

Fashion photography, adults, 113;
  children, 117
Filters, blue, 52–53; green, 98–99;
  yellow, 92–93

Lenses, care, cleaning, 28; telephoto, 60;
  wide angle, 58; zoom, 63

1 Which page would have information about photographing wild animals?

A 1   C 193

B 130   D 216

2 Which page might provide information about using a yellow filter to improve outdoor photography?

J 52   L 98

K 92   M 130

3 Which page might describe how to clean sand from a telephoto lens?

A 19   C 58

B 28   D 63

4 Which page describes the kinds of filters used in color photography?

J 14   L 86

K 18   M 141

5 Which page might discuss how early cameras differed from modern ones?

A 10   C 99

B 28   D 117

STOP

Answers

S1 ● Ⓑ Ⓒ Ⓓ   2 Ⓙ ● Ⓛ Ⓜ   4 Ⓙ Ⓚ Ⓛ ●

1 Ⓐ Ⓑ ● Ⓓ   3 Ⓐ ● Ⓒ Ⓓ   5 ● Ⓑ Ⓒ Ⓓ

Level 12

57

Lesson 25: Using the Dictionary

Directions: Darken the circle for the correct answer.

| TRY THIS | Two guide words appear at the top of each page in a dictionary. They are the first and last words that appear on that particular page. Remember that words are listed in alphabetical order in the dictionary. |

S1

irritable / Italian	376
italic / -ize	377
jab / jackknife	378
jackpot / jasmine	379
jasper / jerky	380

On which page would the word *isthmus* appear?

A 376   C 378
B 377   D 379

 THINK IT THROUGH   The correct answer is A. The "is" in *isthmus* places the word alphabetically between *irritable* and *Italian*, the guide words that appear on page 376.

STOP

Use the guide words in S1 to answer questions 1–6.

1 On which page would the word *jackal* appear?

A 376   C 379
B 378   D 380

4 On which page would the suffix *-ism* appear?

J 376   L 379
K 378   M 380

2 On which page would the word *jeep* appear?

J 376   L 379
K 378   M 380

5 On which page would the word *jamboree* appear?

A 377   C 379
B 378   D 380

3 On which page would the word *isotope* appear?

A 376   C 378
B 377   D 379

6 On which page would the word *ivory* appear?

J 376   L 378
K 377   M 379

GO ON

Level 12

Lesson 25: Using the Dictionary

Study Skills: Using alphabetizing skills with dictionary guide words; obtaining information by interpreting dictionary entries

SAY: **Turn to Lesson 25, Using the Dictionary, on page 58.**

Check to see that all students find Lesson 25.

SAY: **In Lesson 25 you will practice using alphabetizing skills with guide words and getting information from a dictionary by interpreting dictionary entries.**

Read the Directions to students.

SAY: **Now look at Try This.**

Read Try This to students.

SAY: **Now look at S1. Study the list of guide words. Read the question and answer choices carefully. Then darken the circle for the page on which the word *isthmus* would appear.**

Allow students time to find and mark their answer.

SAY: **Now look at Think It Through.**

Read Think It Through to students. Check to see that students have filled in the correct answer space. Ask students if they have any questions.

SAY: **Now you will practice obtaining more information from a dictionary. Do numbers 1 through 11 just as we did S1. When you come to the words *GO ON* at the bottom of a page, continue working on the next page. When you come to the word *STOP* at the bottom of page 59, put your pencils down. You may now begin.**

Allow students time to find and mark their answers.

For questions 7–11, study the sample dictionary and the pronunciation key shown here. Then darken the circle for the correct answer.

mar•i•o•nette (mar ē ə **net′**) *n.* a small jointed figure, made of wood and moved by strings, wires, or rods held from above.

me•di•o•cre (mē dē ō′ kər) *adj.* Not exceptional; ordinary; commonplace.

mi•rage (mi **räzh′**) *n.* An optical illusion caused by the bending of light rays by layers of air having different densities and temperatures.

mis•ad•ven•ture (mis əd ven′ chər) *n.* 1. A mishap. 2. Misfortune.

mis•cast (mis **kast′**) *v.t.* To cast in an unsuitable role: to miscast a comedian as an evil villain.

mo•tor•cade (mō′ tər kād) *n.* A procession of automobiles.

mu•ti•ny (mū′ tə nē) *n.* An open rebellion against authority, especially by sailors or soldiers against their commanding officers.

mys•ti•fy (**mis′** tə fī) *v.t.* To bewilder or confuse; to puzzle.

---

1. Pronunciation Key

a	at	o	hot	ù	pull
ā	ape	ō	old	û	turn
ä	far	ô	song	ch	chin
â	care	ô	fork	ng	sing
e	end	oi	oil	sh	shop
ē	me	ou	out	th	thin
i	it	u	up	th	this
ī	ice	ū	use	hw	in white
î	pierce	ü	rule	zh	in treasure

The ə symbol stands for the unstressed vowel heard in about, taken, pencil, lemon, and circus.

2. Abbreviations: *n.*, noun; *v.*, verb; *adj.* adjective; *pl.*, plural; *v.t.*, transitive verb.

7 How should the word that means "bewilder" be spelled?

A mistafy   C mystifie

B mistifie   D mystify

8 The *y* in mutiny sounds like the *i* in

J marionette.

K misadventure.

L miscast.

M mirage.

9 Which word best fits in the sentence "The director _____ the actor in this movie"?

A mirage   C miscast

B mystify   D mediocre

10 Which sentence correctly uses a form of the word *mirage*?

J We saw a *mirage* as we were driving through the desert.

K The accountant *miraged* the figures in the report.

L The little girl was always getting into *mirage*.

M The *mirage* cakes were very tasty.

11 Which syllable of the word *mediocre* is accented?

A The first   C The third

B The second   D The fourth

STOP

Level 12

59

Answers

7 Ⓐ Ⓑ Ⓒ ●   9 Ⓐ Ⓑ ● Ⓓ   11 Ⓐ Ⓑ ● Ⓓ

8 ● Ⓚ Ⓛ Ⓜ   10 ● Ⓚ Ⓛ Ⓜ

Lesson 26: Using the Library

Directions: Darken the circle for the correct answer.

TRY THIS Carefully study the card from the card catalog. Think about the type of information you are asked to find. Remember that the card catalog has author, title, and subject cards.

SI

ECOLOGY
628   Silverburg, Elizabeth
S   Towards a Cleaner Environment / by Elizabeth Silverburg; photographs by Samantha Richardson; diagrams by John Carlson. —St. Louis: Green Earth Publications Co., 1985 178 p. : illus. : diag. ; 25 cm.
1. Ecology.   2. Recycling.   3. Salvage. I. Title

What does the date 1985 on this card tell you?

A The date the author was born

B The date the publisher started business

C The date the book was published

D The date the library acquired the book

THINK IT THROUGH The correct answer is C. The date 1985 appears after the name of the publishing company. This tells you that it is the date the book was published.

STOP

Use the library catalog card in S1 to answer questions 1 and 2.

1   **What is the title of this book?**

A Ecology

B Green Earth Publications Co.

C Recycling

D Towards a Cleaner Environment

2   **Who is the author of this book?**

J Samantha Richardson

K John Carlson

L Elizabeth Silverburg

M Green Earth Publications Co.

3   **Which of these is best to use to find the definition of the word *zoology*?**

A A dictionary

B A card catalog

C An almanac

D A telephone book

4   **Which of these magazines would be most likely to have up-to-date information about new medical research?**

J *Newsweek*

K *Journal of the American Medical Association*

L *National Geographic*

M *Who's Who in Science*

STOP

Level 12

Answers
S1 Ⓐ Ⓑ ● Ⓓ   2 Ⓙ Ⓚ ● Ⓜ   4 Ⓙ ● Ⓛ Ⓜ
1 Ⓐ Ⓑ Ⓒ ●   3 ● Ⓑ Ⓒ Ⓓ

60

Lesson 26: Using the Library

Study Skills: Choosing appropriate reference materials to gather specific information; using a card catalog

SAY: **Turn to Lesson 26, Using the Library, on page 60.**

Check to see that all students find Lesson 26.

SAY: **In Lesson 26 you will practice interpreting information on a library catalog card and practice determining the appropriate reference material to find certain information.**

Read the Directions to students.

SAY: **Now look at Try This.**

Read Try This to students.

SAY: **Now look at S1. Study the library catalog card. Read the question and answer choices carefully. Then darken the circle for the choice that tells you what the date 1985 on the catalog card means?**

Allow students time to find and mark their answer.

SAY: **Now look at Think It Through.**

Read Think It Through to students. Check to see that students have filled in the correct answer space. Ask students if they have any questions.

SAY: **Now you will practice interpreting more information on a library catalog card and determining the appropriate reference material to find certain information. Do numbers 1 through 4 just as we did S1. When you come to the word *STOP* at the bottom of page 60, put your pencils down. You may now begin.**

Allow students time to find and mark their answers.

Review the questions and answer choices with students. Discuss with the class why one answer is correct and the others are not correct. Also check to see that students have carefully filled in the answer space and have completely erased any stray marks.

Lesson 27: Using Reference Materials

Directions: Darken the circle for the correct answer.

TRY THIS Before you use reference materials, decide which key word or phrase to use to find the information you want.

S1 Which key term should you use to find out about George Washington, Thomas Jefferson, and James Madison?

A United States

B Presidents

C Washington

D Government

THINK IT THROUGH The correct answer is B. George Washington, Thomas Jefferson, and James Madison were all presidents of the United States. To find information about all three, you should use the key word Presidents.

STOP

1 Tornadoes, hurricanes, and cyclones are storms that occur in various parts of the world. **Which key term should you use to find out what causes these storms?**

A Hurricanes C Storms

B Tornadoes D Cyclones

4 A large part of the world's gold supply is mined in Africa. Most of this gold comes from South Africa. **Which key term should you use to find out how gold is mined?**

J Gold L South Africa

K Africa M Mining

2 Many distinctive crafts are produced in Southeast Asia. Batik is a method of making patterns on cloth. **Which key term should you use to find out about this method?**

J Malaysia L Indonesia

K Crafts M Batik

5 The koala is an animal native to Australia. Although referred to as a bear, it is actually a marsupial. **Which key term should you use to find out how the koala meets its need for food?**

A Marsupial C Bear

B Koala D Australia

3 Which key term should you use to find out about the style of French painter Edgar Degas?

A Degas C Art

B France D Painting

6 Which key term should you use to learn about the amount of annual rainfall in Chile?

J Precipitation L Chile

K Rainfall M Climate

STOP

Level 12

Answers

S1 Ⓐ ● Ⓒ Ⓓ 2 Ⓙ Ⓚ Ⓛ ● 4 ● Ⓚ Ⓛ Ⓜ 6 Ⓙ Ⓚ ● Ⓜ

1 Ⓐ Ⓑ ● Ⓓ 3 ● Ⓑ Ⓒ Ⓓ 5 Ⓐ ● Ⓒ Ⓓ

61

Lesson 27: Using Reference Materials

Study Skill: Identifying key terms to locate appropriate reference material to find specific information

SAY: **Turn to Lesson 27, Using Reference Materials, on page 61.**

Check to see that all students find Lesson 27.

SAY: **In Lesson 27 you will practice identifying key terms to use to find information in an appropriate reference source.**

Read the Directions to students.

SAY: **Now look at Try This.**

Read Try This to students.

SAY: **Now look at S1. Read the question and answer choices carefully. Then darken the circle for the key term you would use to find out about George Washington, Thomas Jefferson, and James Madison.**

Allow students time to find and mark their answer.

SAY: **Now look at Think It Through.**

Read Think It Through to students. Check to see that students have filled in the correct answer space. Ask students if they have any questions.

SAY: **Now you will practice identifying more key terms to use to find information in an appropriate reference source. Do numbers 1 through 6 just as we did S1. When you come to the word _STOP_ at the bottom of page 61, put your pencils down. You may now begin.**

Allow students time to find and mark their answers.

Review the questions and answer choices with students. Discuss with the class why one answer is correct and the others are not correct. Also check to see that students have carefully filled in the answer space and have completely erased any stray marks.

Unit 10 Test

S1 Which of these would show the best route to take from Detroit to Kansas City?

    A An atlas

    B A language book

    C A dictionary

    D A newspaper

STOP

For questions 1–18, darken the circle for the correct answer.

Use the index below to answer questions 1–5.

INDEX

Accidents, first aid, 20; prevention, 24; bandages, 27

Campfires, controlling, 16; cooking, 19; extinguishing, 17; starting, 15

Clothes, boots, 131; for cold weather, 137; gloves, 133; hiking shoes, 136

Food, cereal, 83; dried fruit, 85; meats, 87; vegetables, 89; *See also* Recipes

Mountain camping, 118

Plants, edible, 95–98; poisonous, 91–94

Recipes, 173–180; eggs, 177; hamburger, 175

Safety and first aid, 43–81; bee sting, 44; bleeding, 61; burns, 71; snake bite, 79

Tents, canvas, 37; nylon, 39

Tools, axes, 29; for mountain climbing, 31; for tents, 35–36; hammers, 32

---

1 Which page might describe the kind of clothing needed for cold-weather camping?

    A 136

    B 137

    C 131

    D 133

2 Which page might explain how to treat a bee sting?

    J 24

    K 27

    L 44

    M 79

3 Which page might describe poisonous forest plants?

    A 85

    B 89

    C 91

    D 95

4 Which page might tell what tools are needed to pitch a tent?

    J 29

    K 35

    L 39

    M 68

5 Which page might explain how to make a hamburger while camping?

    A 89

    B 175

    C 177

    D 32

GO ON

Level 12

Answers

S1 ● Ⓑ Ⓒ Ⓓ   2 Ⓙ Ⓚ ● Ⓜ   4 Ⓙ ● Ⓛ Ⓜ

62 1 Ⓐ ● Ⓒ Ⓓ   3 Ⓐ Ⓑ ● Ⓓ   5 Ⓐ ● Ⓒ Ⓓ

Unit 10 Test

SAY: **Turn to the Unit 10 Test on page 62.**

Check to see that all students find the Unit 10 Test.

SAY: **In this test you will use the study skills that we have practiced in this unit. Look at S1. You are asked to identify the reference source to use to find the best route to take from Detroit to Kansas City. Darken the circle for the correct answer.**

Allow students time to find and mark their answer.

SAY: **You should have darkened the circle for *A*. An *atlas* is the best reference source to use to find travel routes between locations.**

Check to see that all students have filled in the correct answer space. Ask students if they have any questions.

SAY: **Now you will finish the test on your own. Do numbers 1 through 18 just as we did S1. Read the questions and answer choices carefully. Then darken the circle for each correct answer. When you come to the words *GO ON* at the bottom of a page, continue working on the next page. When you come to the word *STOP* at the bottom of page 64, put your pencils down. You may now begin.**

Allow students time to find and mark their answers.

Use the sample dictionary and the pronunciation key below to answer questions 6–8.

fade (fād) *v.* **1.** To lose color or brightness. **2.** To lose freshness or appeal. **3.** To disappear gradually.

fin•er•y (fī′ nə rē) *n.* Fine or showy clothes or ornaments.

fi•nesse (fi **nes**′) *n.* **1.** Refinement or skill in doing something. **2.** The smooth or skillful handling of an awkward or difficult situation.

flo•rist (**flôr**′ ist) *n.* A person who raises or sells flowers and plants.

fran•tic (**fran**′ tik) *adj.* Wildly excited by grief, worry, fear, or anger.

fur•tive (**fûr**′ tiv) *adj.* **1.** Done by stealth; secret. **2.** Shifty; sly.

---

1. Pronunciation Key

a	at	o	hot	u̇	pull
ā	ape	ō	old	û	turn
ä	far	ô	song	ch	chin
â	care	ô	fork	ng	sing
e	end	oi	oil	sh	shop
ē	me	ou	out	th	thin
i	it	u	up	th	this
ī	ice	ū	use	hw	in white
î	pierce	ü	rule	zh	in treasure

The ə symbol stands for the unstressed vowel heard in **a**bout, tak**e**n, penc**i**l, lem**o**n, and circ**u**s.

2. Abbreviations: *n.*, noun; *v.*, verb; *adj.* adjective; *pl.*, plural.

---

6 Which word describes a skill you might need as a diplomat?

  J finery   **L** florist
  K finesse   **M** frantic

7 Which sentence correctly uses a form of the word *frantic*?

  A My friend came to school dressed in *frantic*.
  B She became *frantic* when she lost her house keys.
  C She was so happy she was *frantic*.
  D The *frantic* bus had a flat tire.

8 When *d* is added, which of these words becomes an adjective?

  J florist
  K finery
  L furtive
  M fade

Use the dictionary guide words shown here to answer questions 9 and 10.

my /mythology	469
nag / nap	470
napkin / native	471
natural / navel	472
navigate / Nebraska	473

9 On which page would you find the word *mystery*?

  A 469   **C** 472
  B 471   **D** 473

10 On which page would you find the word *nautical*?

  J 470   **L** 472
  K 471   **M** 473

GO ON

Use the following card from a library card catalog to answer questions 11–13.

AMERICAN FLAG

712.0 Rider, Emily J.

R   History of the American Flag /
        by Emily J. Rider;
        photographs by Bob Patterson.
        —Bishop City, Iowa: American Press,
        1990.
        323 p. : illus.

        1. American History 2. Flags.
        3. American Flag. I. Title.

11 **What is the title of this book?**

  A American History

  B Flags

  C American Flag

  D History of the American Flag

12 **Who is Bob Patterson?**

  J The editor of the book

  K The author of the book

  L The person who published the book

  M The person who took the photographs in the book

13 **Who published the book?**

  A American Press

  B Emily J. Rider

  C Bob Patterson

  D Bishop City

14 **Which of these would tell you about the history of Spain?**

  J A dictionary

  K An encyclopedia

  L A newspaper

  M An atlas

15 **Which of these would tell you the meaning of the word *mirth*?**

  A An encyclopedia

  B A dictionary

  C A language book

  D A social studies book

For questions 16–18, darken the circle for the correct answer.

16 A healthy diet contains the right amount of six types of nutrients: fats, carbohydrates, proteins, water, minerals, and vitamins. **Which key term should you use to find out where the nutrients are found?**

  J Health

  K Balanced diet

  L Food

  M Nutrients

17 **Which key term should you use to find out about the difference between the winter wheat and summer wheat grown in the Midwest?**

  A Midwest

  B Winter

  C Summer

  D Wheat

18 **Which key word should you use to find out about the eruptions of famous volcanoes, such as Mount Etna in Sicily and Mount Saint Helens in the United States?**

  J Eruptions

  K Volcano

  L Sicily

  M United States

STOP

Level 12

Answers

64

11 Ⓐ Ⓑ Ⓒ ●   13 ● Ⓑ Ⓒ Ⓓ   15 Ⓐ ● Ⓒ Ⓓ   17 Ⓐ Ⓑ Ⓒ ●

12 Ⓙ Ⓚ Ⓛ ●   14 Ⓙ ● Ⓛ Ⓜ   16 Ⓙ Ⓚ Ⓛ ●   18 Ⓙ ● Ⓛ Ⓜ

SAY: **It is now time to stop. You have completed the Unit 10 Test. Make sure that you have carefully filled in your answer spaces and have completely erased any stray marks. Then put your pencils down.**

After the test has been scored, review the questions and answer choices with students. If students are having difficulty, provide them with additional practice.

Test Best Comprehensive Tests

Getting Ready for the Comprehensive Tests

The Comprehensive Tests are designed to simulate the Iowa Tests of Basic Skills. Each Comprehensive Test has a recommended time limit. It is suggested that you follow these time limits and that you schedule no more than four tests in one day, providing sufficient breaks between tests.

Following the suggestions presented here will enable students to experience test taking under the same structured conditions that apply when achievement tests are administered. Furthermore, students will have a final opportunity to apply the skills they have learned in *Test Best*, prior to taking the Iowa Tests Of Basic Skills.

The following table lists recommended test sessions and time limits for each test. It is suggested that you allow fifteen or twenty minutes for students to complete the personal information required on the *Test Best* Answer Sheet shown on pages 80 and 81 of this book and on pages 93 and 94 of the student book.

Test Session	Comprehensive Test	Test Time
First Day	1—Vocabulary	15
	2—Reading Comprehension	25
	3—Spelling	10
Second Day	4—Language Mechanics	15
	5—Language Expression	20
	6—Math Concepts and Estimation	20
Third Day	7—Math Problems	20
	8—Math Computation	10
	9—Maps and Diagrams	20
	10—Reference Materials	20

Test Day

To simulate the structured atmosphere of the Iowa Tests of Basic Skills, take the following steps on the day of the test:

- Hang a "Do Not Disturb—Testing" sign on the classroom door to avoid interruptions.

- Use a stopwatch to accurately observe the time limit marked on each test.

- Remove the Answer Sheet (found on pages 93 and 94) from each *Test Best on the Iowa Tests of Basic Skills* book.

- Seat students at an appropriate distance from one another, and make sure that their desks are clear of all materials.

- Provide students with sharpened pencils that have erasers.

- Keep supplies, such as extra pencils and scratch paper for Tests 6, 7, and 8, readily available.

- Distribute the *Test Best* books to students, and encourage them to do their best.

Before you begin, remind students to press firmly with their pencils to make a dark mark. Remind students of the importance of completely filling in the answer spaces and erasing any stray marks that might be picked up as answers by the scoring machines.

While you are administering the Comprehensive Tests, make sure that students understand the directions before proceeding with each test. Circulate around the classroom, making sure that students are following the directions, that they are working on the appropriate test, and that they are marking their Answer Sheets properly. Check to see that students have carefully filled in the answer spaces and have completely erased any stray marks.

Answer Sheet

STUDENT'S NAME

LAST   FIRST   MI

SCHOOL:

TEACHER:

FEMALE ○   MALE ○

BIRTH DATE

MONTH	DAY	YEAR
Jan ○	⓪ ⓪	⓪ ⓪
Feb ○	① ①	① ①
Mar ○	② ②	② ②
Apr ○	③ ③	③ ③
May ○	④	④ ④
Jun ○	⑤	⑤ ⑤
Jul ○	⑥	⑥ ⑥
Aug ○	⑦	⑦ ⑦
Sep ○	⑧	⑧ ⑧
Oct ○	⑨	⑨ ⑨
Nov ○		
Dec ○		

GRADE   ③ ④ ⑤ ⑥ ⑦ ⑧

TEST BEST
ON THE
IOWA TESTS OF BASIC SKILLS®

Iowa Tests of Basic Skills® is a trademark of the Riverside Publishing Company. Such company has neither endorsed nor authorized this test-preparation book.

TEST 1   Vocabulary

S1 Ⓐ ● Ⓒ Ⓓ

TEST 2   Reading Comprehension

S1 ● Ⓑ Ⓒ Ⓓ

TEST 3   Spelling

S1 Ⓐ Ⓑ Ⓒ Ⓓ ●

Level 12   **93**

CUT HERE

Preparing the *Test Best* Answer Sheet

Distribute a *Test Best* Answer Sheet to each student. Refer to the *Test Best* Answer Sheet shown on this page and have students complete the required personal data. Use the procedures below to properly mark the personal data on the Answer Sheet. This will help ensure that students' test results will be properly recorded.

SAY: **Before we begin with Test 1 of the Comprehensive Tests, we need to complete some information on the *Test Best* Answer Sheet. We will do this together now. Make sure that you are looking at page 93, with the heading *STUDENT'S NAME* at the top of the page. Just below this at the left is the heading *LAST*. In the boxes under *LAST*, print your last name—one letter in each box. Print as many letters as will fit. In the boxes under *FIRST*, print your first name—one letter in each box. Print as many letters as will fit. If you have a middle name, print your middle initial in the *MI* box. Leave the *MI* box empty if you do not have a middle name.**

Allow students time to print their names.

SAY: **Now look at the columns of letters below each of the boxes. In each column, darken the circle that matches the letter in that box. Darken the empty circle at the top of the column if there is no letter in the box.**

Allow students time to darken the circles. Circulate around the classroom to make sure that students are completing the appropriate part of the Answer Sheet.

SAY: **Now look at the top right side of your Answer Sheet where it lists *SCHOOL* and *TEACHER*.**

Print the school's name and your name on the chalkboard and allow students time to copy this information onto their Answer Sheets.

TEST 4 — Language Mechanics

S1 A B ● D S2 ● K L M
1 ● B C D
2 J ● L M
3 A B C ●
4 J K ● M
5 A ● C D
6 J K ● M
7 ● B C D
8 ● K L M
9 A B ● D
10 J ● L M
11 A ● C D
12 J K ● M
13 ● B C D
14 J K L ●
15 A B C ●
16 J ● L M
17 A B ● D
18 J ● L M
19 A B ● D
20 ● K L M
21 A B ● D
22 ● K L M
23 A ● C D
24 J ● L M

TEST 5 — Language Expression

S1 A B ● D
1 A B ● D
2 J ● L M
3 ● B C D
4 ● K L M
5 ● B C D
6 J ● L M
7 A ● C D
8 ● K L M
9 A B C ●
10 J K ● M
11 ● B C D
12 J K ● M
13 ● B C D
14 J ● L M
15 A B ● D
16 J K L ●
17 ● B C D
18 J K L ●
19 ● B C D
20 J K ● M
21 A B C ●
22 ● K L M
23 A ● C D
24 J K L ●
25 ● B C D
26 ● K L M
27 A B ● D
28 ● K L M
29 ● B C D
30 J K L ●
31 A ● C D
32 J ● L M

TEST 6 — Math Concepts and Estimation

S1 A ● C D
1 A B C ●
2 ● K L M
3 ● B C D
4 ● K L M
5 A ● C D
6 J K L ●
7 A ● C D
8 J K ● M
9 A B ● D
10 J ● L M
11 A B ● D
12 ● K L M
13 A B ● D
14 J K ● M
15 ● B C D
16 ● K L M
17 ● B C D
18 J K ● M
19 ● B C D
20 J K L ●
21 A B ● D
22 ● K L M
23 A B ● D
24 J ● L M
25 A B C ●
26 J K L ●
27 A ● C D
28 J ● L M
29 ● B C D
30 ● K L M
31 A B ● D

TEST 7 — Math Problems

S1 A ● C D
1 A B ● D
2 J ● L M
3 ● B C D
4 J K L ●
5 ● B C D
6 J K L ●
7 A B C ●
8 J K ● M
9 A B C ●
10 J ● L M
11 A B ● D
12 J ● L M
13 A B C ●
14 ● K L M
15 A B ● D
16 ● K L M
17 A B C ●
18 J ● L M
19 A ● C D
20 J ● L M

TEST 8 — Math Computation

S1 A B ● D S2 J ● L M
1 A ● C D
2 J K ● M
3 A ● C D
4 ● K L M
5 A ● C D
6 ● K L M
7 ● B C D
8 J ● L M
9 A ● C D
10 J K ● M

TEST 9 — Maps and Diagrams

S1 A B ● D
1 A ● C D
2 J K ● M
3 ● B C D
4 ● K L M
5 A ● C D
6 J K L ●
7 ● B C D
8 J ● L M
9 A B C ●
10 J K ● M
11 A B ● D
12 J K L ●
13 A ● C D
14 ● K L M
15 A B C ●
16 J K ● M
17 A B ● D
18 J K L ●

TEST 10 — Reference Materials

S1 A B ● D
1 A B ● D
2 J K L ●
3 A ● C D
4 ● K L M
5 A B ● D
6 ● K L M
7 A B C ●
8 J ● L M
9 A B C ●
10 ● K L M
11 A ● C D
12 ● K L M
13 A ● C D
14 J K ● M
15 ● B C D
16 J ● L M
17 A ● C D
18 J ● L M
19 A B C ●
20 J ● L M
21 A B ● D
22 J ● L M

ISBN 0-8114-2863-X
90000
9 780811 428637

CUT HERE

SAY: **Now look at the section directly below *TEACHER*. Darken the circle for *FEMALE* if you are a girl. Darken the circle for *MALE* if you are a boy. Then look at the *BIRTH DATE* section. Under *MONTH*, darken the circle for the month you were born. Under *DAY*, darken the circles that have the one or two numerals of the day you were born. If your birthday has only one numeral, darken the circle for zero in the first column of numerals. Under *YEAR* darken the circles for the last two numbers of the year you were born. Finally, under *GRADE*, darken the circle that has the number for your grade.**

Allow students time to complete the information. Remind students to press firmly on their pencils to make a dark mark. Check to see that students have carefully filled in the circles and have completely erased any stray marks. Remind students of the importance of completely filling the answer space and erasing any stray marks that might be picked up as answers by the scoring machines.

Comprehensive Tests

Test 1: Vocabulary

S1   **Accept** a gift
- A give
- B receive
- C buy
- D sell

STOP

For questions 1–28, darken the circle for the word or words that mean the same or almost the same as the word in dark type.

1   A **bare** cupboard
- A empty
- B clean
- C dirty
- D full

2   A **colossal** statue
- J marble
- K broken
- L ordinary
- M huge

3   **Employ** an assistant
- A hire
- B want
- C replace
- D purchase

4   **Demonstrate** the new computer
- J adjust
- K turn off
- L show
- M package

5   **Bind** the packages
- A open
- B send
- C receive
- D secure

6   The **core** of the earth
- J crust
- K center
- L atmosphere
- M axis

7   To **incline** toward
- A lean
- B invade
- C support
- D vary

8   A **notorious** spy
- J bothersome
- K destructive
- L well-known
- M beginning

9   Disobey the **ordinance**
- A law
- B conference
- C parent
- D judge

10   **Prune** the fruit tree
- J plant
- K throw out
- L trim
- M light

11   An **expensive** car
- A costly
- B foreign
- C excellent
- D fast

12   An **actual** fort
- J acute
- K ancient
- L real
- M strong

13   A **spare** tire
- A extra
- B rubber
- C flat
- D worn

GO ON

Level 12

65

Comprehensive Tests

Test 1: Vocabulary

Allow 15 minutes for this test.

SAY: **Turn to Test 1, Vocabulary, on page 65.**

Check to see that all students find Test 1.

SAY: **In this test you will use your vocabulary skills to answer questions. Look at S1. Read the phrase and answer choices carefully. Then darken the circle for the correct answer.**

Allow students time to find and mark their answer.

SAY: **You should have darkened the circle for _B_. The word _receive_ means the same or almost the same as the word in dark type, _Accept_.**

Check to see that all students have filled in the correct answer space. Ask students if they have any questions.

SAY: **Now you will finish the test on your own. Read the directions carefully. Then do numbers 1 through 28 just as we did S1. Darken the circle for each correct answer. When you come to the words _GO ON_ at the bottom of page 65, continue working on the next page. When you come to the word _STOP_ at the bottom of page 66, put your pencils down. You have 15 minutes to complete the test. You may now begin.**

Allow students 15 minutes to find and mark their answers.

14 **Astonish** the audience
  J frighten
  K welcome
  L amaze
  M cheat

15 **Eliminate** the light
  A get rid of
  B increase
  C turn on
  D decrease

16 To **embezzle** the funds
  J count
  K steal
  L clean
  M sort

17 To **occupy** space
  A uncover
  B inhabit
  C exhaust
  D analyze

18 Mail the **parcel**
  J jacket
  K letter
  L suitcase
  M package

19 A **futile** attempt
  A successful
  B worthless
  C rewarding
  D nervous

20 To **govern** wisely
  J violate
  K profit
  L invest
  M rule

21 A yearly **donation**
  A bill
  B gift
  C visit
  D party

22 A **pessimistic** outlook
  J gloomy
  K bright
  L corrupt
  M confident

23 A **courteous** manner
  A affectionate
  B strict
  C polite
  D reliable

24 A beautiful **fabric**
  J cloth
  K fable
  L dress
  M nylon

25 In **opposition** to
  A resistance
  B definition
  C cooperation
  D agreement

26 A large **yacht**
  J limousine
  K airplane
  L ship
  M blimp

27 Clearly **audible**
  A indistinct
  B capable of being heard
  C intelligent
  D unprepared

28 The bus **terminal**
  J battery
  K station
  L route
  M driver

STOP
Level 12

SAY: **It is now time to stop. You have completed Test 1. Make sure that you have carefully filled in your answer spaces and have completely erased any stray marks. Then put your pencils down and close your books.**

After the test has been scored, review the questions and answer choices with students. If students are having difficulty, provide them with additional practice items.

Test 2: Reading Comprehension

S1　Cindy often helps her father with the household chores. She sorts the clothes before they are washed. She cleans the bird's cage. Sometimes she vacuums her room.

What does Cindy do before the clothes are washed?

A　She sorts the clothes.

B　She cleans the bird's cage.

C　She folds the clothes.

D　She vacuums her room.

STOP

For questions 1–23, read each selection carefully. Then darken the circle for the correct answer to each question.

Many brightly colored lights are made from a gas called neon. Neon is one of many gases in the earth's atmosphere. About 80 years ago, Georges Claude, a French chemist, found a way to use neon to make lights. He took the air out of a glass tube and replaced it with neon. When electricity was passed through the neon, a very colorful light was created.

You have probably seen neon lights in restaurant signs or on highways. Airports sometimes use neon lights to guide airplanes because neon can be seen through thick fog. Some people use neon signs in their businesses and offices. Some pieces of art are made of neon lights.

Some signs look just like those that use neon, but they use other gases. Argon is another gas used in signs. It gives off a lavender color. Neon gives off an orange-red color. Even though different gases may be used, people always call the signs neon signs.

1　**What is neon?**

A　A gas used to make signs

B　A brightly colored sign

C　A kind of electricity

D　A thick fog

2　**Why are neon lights used at airports?**

J　They are colorful.

K　They can be seen through thick fog.

L　They are used to light airport restaurants.

M　They are inexpensive.

3　**How is argon like neon?**

A　It gives off the same color.

B　It was also discovered by Georges Claude.

C　It is a gas.

D　It is a kind of sign.

4　**The main purpose of this passage is**

J　to describe various kinds of neon signs.

K　to convince us that neon is better than electricity.

L　to advertise neon lights.

M　to present information about neon.

GO ON

Level 12

67

Test 2: Reading Comprehension

Allow 25 minutes for this test.

SAY: **Turn to Test 2, Reading Comprehension, on page 67.**

Check to see that all students find Test 2.

SAY: **In this test you will use your reading skills to answer questions about selections that you read. Look at S1. Read the selection, the question, and the answer choices carefully. Then darken the circle for the correct answer.**

Allow students time to find and mark their answer.

SAY: **You should have darkened the circle for _A_ because the selection states that Cindy sorts the clothes before they are washed.**

Check to see that all students have filled in the correct answer space. Ask students if they have any questions.

SAY: **Now you will finish the test on your own. Do questions 1 through 23 just as we did S1. Darken the circle for each correct answer. When you come to the words _GO ON_ at the bottom of a page, continue working on the next page. When you come to the word _STOP_ at the bottom of page 71, put your pencils down. You have 25 minutes to complete the test. You may now begin.**

Allow students 25 minutes to find and mark their answers.

Frieda and her mother lived in an apartment in New York City. Frieda had no brothers or sisters, and there were no children living nearby. Her best friend was a very old woman named Maria, who lived down the hall.

Maria's most prized possessions were a cat named Javier and an album of photographs from her family in Costa Rica. When she visited Maria, Frieda liked to study the album. Men in big mustaches and women in embroidered blouses stared from the photographs. Maria would begin by talking about these long-dead relatives but would end by telling stories about the jaguars and parrots that lived in the rain forest near her family home. Frieda loved listening to these stories. She wanted to become a scientist to help save the rain forests from destruction.

One night as Frieda was doing her homework she heard sirens, and fire trucks suddenly appeared on the street below. The next thing she knew, a firefighter was pounding on their door. The top floors of the building were on fire. Frieda's mother shouted, "Grab your stereo and let's go!" Frieda had saved her money for a year to buy the stereo.

"Maria may need help," Frieda yelled as she raced down the hall to her friend's apartment. The door was standing open. The firefighters had already helped Maria and Javier downstairs. Frieda grabbed the heavy photo album from the shelf where Maria always kept it. Frieda hurried downstairs; smoke was filling the hallways.

Frieda's mother was anxiously waiting for her on the street. She saw that her daughter had saved only Maria's photo album. "I'm sorry about your stereo," Frieda's mother said.

"That's all right," Frieda said, "I made the right choice."

GO ON

5 The story takes place in

A Costa Rica.

B the country.

C a tropical rain forest.

D New York City.

6 Why did Frieda like to visit Maria?

J To play with her cat, Javier

K To feed the parrots and jaguars

L To talk about the day at school

M To see pictures of Maria's relatives

7 Why did Frieda want to become a scientist?

A To find a cure for cancer

B To become rich and famous

C To have a better life for herself and her mother

D To save the rain forests from destruction

8 Maria's most prized possessions were an album of photographs and

J a collection of postcards.

K a parrot from Brazil.

L a cat named Javier.

M a grandfather clock.

9 In this selection, the word "embroidered" means

A decorated with fancy raised designs made with thread.

B dry clean only.

C made in Costa Rica.

D smooth-textured, imported fabric.

10 When did Frieda hurry downstairs?

J When the firefighters pounded on her door

K Before she saw the fire truck

L After she grabbed Maria's album

M When she saw Maria and her cat

11 Why did Frieda grab the photo album?

A She knew it meant a lot to Maria.

B She always wanted to own it.

C She did not see anything else to save.

D Maria told her to save it.

12 This selection is mostly about a girl who

J fights a fire.

K makes a difficult choice.

L saves her own favorite thing.

M knows how to save money.

13 What did Frieda mean by "I made the right choice"?

A The album cost more than the stereo.

B Maria could never replace the album.

C Maria would give her a reward.

D She was tired of her stereo.

14 Which of these would be the best title for this selection?

J "Frieda Saves for a Stereo"

K "Maria and Javier"

L "The Deadly Fire"

M "Frieda's Choice"

GO ON

My sixth-grade class was about to take a field trip to the Museum of Science and Industry. The museum has about 2,000 exhibits located in its 75 exhibit halls. There are too many exhibits to see all in one day. As a result my teacher, Mr. Keller, decided to prepare us for the trip. He wanted us to know exactly where we would be going and what we were going to see.

First, Mr. Keller divided the class into groups of four or five students and gave each group a map of the museum. Mr. Keller explained that we would remain in the same groups for our field trip. Second, each group was instructed to make a list of twenty-five exhibits they would like to see. Next, we were asked to list the ten exhibits we would most like to see. Finally, Mr. Keller asked the groups to use their maps to arrange their day based on the locations of the top ten exhibits. He explained that we would see more exhibits if we moved around the museum in an orderly manner. If we had time left after we saw our top ten choices, we could go back to our original list. He told us that we would have about six hours to tour the museum and half an hour for lunch.

My group followed Mr. Keller's instructions. Our list of ten exhibits included historic trains, a space shuttle experience, cycle works, a submarine tour, cars of yesteryear, a fairy castle, a working coal mine, the money center, the whispering gallery, and the heart. After we had decided on our list, we looked at our map to locate the exhibits. The first five exhibits were on the first floor. We decided to try to see all these exhibits before lunch. Then we would head for the cafeteria, also located on the first floor. After lunch we would go to the third floor to see our sixth and seventh choices. Then we would go to the second floor to see our last three choices. We allowed two hours to tour each floor.

I am glad that Mr. Keller had us prepare for our visit to the museum. Everyone in the class is excited to go to the museum knowing that they will see their favorite exhibits. I can hardly wait to tour the submarine.

GO ON

Level 12

70

15 How many exhibits does the Museum of Science and Industry have?

A 2,000

B 200

C 75

D 25

16 According to the selection, the first thing Mr. Keller did to prepare his class for the field trip was to

J read an article to the class about the museum.

K show the class a videotape about the museum.

L ask the students to write reports about other visits to the museum.

M divide the class into groups and give each group a map of the museum.

17 What did Mr. Keller ask his students to do after they made a list of twenty-five exhibits they would like to see?

A Arrange their day based on the locations of the twenty-five exhibits they had chosen

B List the ten exhibits they would most like to see

C Decide which cafeteria they would like to go to for lunch

D Write a report about each of the exhibits

18 According to the author, which of the following exhibits made the list of ten exhibits of the author's group?

J Ships through the ages

K The doll collection

L Cars of yesteryear

M Seagoing vessels

19 Which of the following exhibits is located on the first floor of the museum?

A The heart

B A fairy castle

C A space shuttle experience

D The money center

20 The museum cafeteria was located

J in the basement.

K on the first floor.

L on the second floor.

M on the third floor.

21 You can conclude from this selection that the students would probably

A misbehave at the museum.

B not know where to go for lunch at the museum.

C see all the exhibits at the museum.

D see at least ten exhibits at the museum.

22 This selection is mostly about

J writing a report about a science museum.

K planning a day at a science museum.

L a student's review of a science museum.

M a bus trip to a science museum.

23 According to the selection, the author expects to

A spend all of the day on the first floor of the museum.

B be bored most of the day at the science museum.

C tour the submarine and the heart exhibit.

D get lost in the museum.

STOP

Level 12

71

After the test has been scored, review the questions and answer choices with students. If students are having difficulty, provide them with additional practice items.

Test 3: Spelling

S1
A fossil
B arc
C internal
D occupant
E *(No mistakes)*

STOP

For questions 1–16, darken the circle for the word that is **not** spelled correctly. Darken the circle for *No mistakes* if all the words are spelled correctly.

1
A comittee
B complicate
C combat
D compete
E *(No mistakes)*

2
J intrigue
K surgon
L mammal
M evident
N *(No mistakes)*

3
A applause
B cautious
C thankfull
D potent
E *(No mistakes)*

4
J signature
K vaccination
L political
M scholare
N *(No mistakes)*

5
A jagged
B ovious
C memorize
D luggage
E *(No mistakes)*

6
J mischivous
K finally
L missile
M opinion
N *(No mistakes)*

7
A disgise
B smudge
C embarrassment
D debtor
E *(No mistakes)*

8
J transparent
K magnificent
L delegate
M instructer
N *(No mistakes)*

9
A agression
B handicap
C spectator
D chord
E *(No mistakes)*

10
J catalog
K streak
L wrestel
M macaroni
N *(No mistakes)*

11
A surgery
B neglect
C description
D advokate
E *(No mistakes)*

12
J bouquet
K desimal
L embankment
M anticipate
N *(No mistakes)*

13
A senior
B vicinity
C dominoes
D vacume
E *(No mistakes)*

14
J involve
K invoice
L inward
M iodine
N *(No mistakes)*

15
A individual
B leadership
C balconi
D treatment
E *(No mistakes)*

16
J helmet
K nugget
L democrattic
M rotten
N *(No mistakes)*

STOP

Level 12

Test 3: Spelling

Allow 10 minutes for this test.

SAY: **Turn to Test 3, Spelling, on page 72.**

Check to see that all students find Test 3.

SAY: **In this test you will use your language skills to find the correct spellings of words. Look at S1. Read the answer choices carefully. Then darken the circle for the correct answer.**

Allow students time to find and mark their answer.

SAY: **You should have darkened the circle for *E* because all of the words are spelled correctly.**

Check to see that all students have filled in the correct answer space. Ask students if they have any questions.

SAY: **Now you will finish the test on your own. Read the directions carefully. Then do numbers 1 through 16 just as we did S1. Darken the circle for each correct answer. When you come to the word *STOP* at the bottom of page 72, put your pencils down. You have 10 minutes to complete the test. You may now begin.**

Allow students 10 minutes to find and mark their answers.

SAY: **It is now time to stop. You have completed Test 3. Make sure that you have carefully filled in your answer spaces and have completely erased any stray marks. Then put your pencils down and close your books.**

After the test has been scored, review the questions and answer choices with students. If students are having difficulty, provide them with additional practice.

Test 4: Language Mechanics

Test 4: Language Mechanics

S1 A Last year my best friend moved
    B from Rochester, New York,
    C to Little rock, Arkansas.
    D *(No mistakes)*

STOP

S2 J Do you ride a bicycle If you
    K do, then you should be familiar
    L with bicycle safety rules.
    M *(No mistakes)*

STOP

For questions 1–11, darken the circle for the line that has a capitalization error. If there are no capitalization errors, darken the circle for *No mistakes.*

1 A The seventh-grade Math teacher
   B at Milburn Middle School has
   C taught for more than ten years.
   D *(No mistakes)*

2 J "Hurry!" yelled my mother.
   K "we will be late for the
   L first act of the play."
   M *(No mistakes)*

3 A My grandmother lives in
   B an old house on Douglas
   C Street in Salt Lake City.
   D *(No mistakes)*

4 J I will be going to camp for the
   K first time next summer. Luis
   L will be my Counselor.
   M *(No mistakes)*

5 A Yuri's favorite holiday is the
   B fourth of July. He likes to watch
   C fireworks with his family.
   D *(No mistakes)*

6 J As a child, one of my favorite
   K bedtime stories was "Snow White
   L and the seven dwarfs."
   M *(No mistakes)*

7 A Maine was owned by an english
   B family before it became one of
   C the original 13 colonies.
   D *(No mistakes)*

8 J   381 Sandy Grove lane
   K   Charlotte, NC 27321
   L   May 15, 1995
   M *(No mistakes)*

9 A Chadwick Furniture Co.
   B Greensboro, NC 27345
   C dear Sales Manager:
   D *(No mistakes)*

10 J Please send me your most
   K recent Catalog featuring your
   L new line of outdoor furniture.
   M *(No mistakes)*

11 A I have enclosed $1.00 for postage.
   B   sincerely,
   C   *Mary Willis*
   D *(No mistakes)*

GO ON

Level 12

Test 4: Language Mechanics

Allow 15 minutes for this test.

SAY: **Turn to Test 4, Language Mechanics, on page 73.**

Check to see that all students find Test 4.

SAY: **In this test you will use your language skills to identify errors in capitalization and punctuation and to find correct capitalization and punctuation. Look at S1. Read the lines carefully. Then darken the circle for the line that has a capitalization error.**

Allow students time to find and mark their answer.

SAY: **You should have darkened the circle for *C* because the name of a city is always capitalized.**

Check to see that all students have filled in the correct answer space. Ask students if they have any questions.

SAY: **Now look at S2. Read the lines carefully. Then darken the circle for the line that has a punctuation error.**

Allow students time to find and mark their answer.

SAY: **You should have darkened the circle for *J* because a sentence always ends with a punctuation mark.**

Check to see that all students have filled in the correct answer space. Ask students if they have any questions.

SAY: **Now you will finish the test on your own. Read the directions for each section carefully. Then do questions 1 through 24 just as we did the samples. Darken the circle for each correct answer. When you come to the words *GO ON* at the bottom of page 73, continue working on the next page. When you come to the word *STOP* at the bottom of page 74, put your pencils down. You have 15 minutes to complete the test. You may now begin.**

For questions 12–24, darken the circle for the line that has a punctuation error. If there are no punctuation errors, darken the circle for *No mistakes.*

12 J Rachel asked, "What do
   K you get when you
   L multiply 54 by 45"
   M *(No mistakes)*

13 A I wrote ten letters' to my
   B friends while I was at camp.
   C I received only five replies.
   D *(No mistakes)*

14 J Jon asked to borrow my
   K camera. I lent it to him
   L with new batteries and film.
   M *(No mistakes)*

15 A My cousin, who lives in Florida,
   B collects seashells from around
   C the world. His collection is huge.
   D *(No mistakes)*

16 J Carl and his friend Rafael
   K wanted to go to the movies. Carls
   L father drove them to the theater.
   M *(No mistakes)*

17 A "Welcome to my birthday party,"
   B said Lin. "Are you thirsty? We
   C have water, milk, and diet, soda."
   D *(No mistakes)*

18 J My family always has a
   K wonderful time, when Aunt
   L Beatrice comes to stay with us.
   M *(No mistakes)*

19 A Some visitors to the state of Texas
   B are surprised to find mountains,
   C beaches forests and plains.
   D *(No mistakes)*

20 J Yesterday, a song written by
   K the Beatles, has been recorded
   L by dozens of musicians.
   M *(No mistakes)*

21 A   9832 South Congress Ave.
   B   Jacksonville, TX 78641
   C   January 19 1995
   D *(No mistakes)*

22 J Great Plains Publishing Co.,
   K Cheyenne, WY 80076
   L Dear Editor:
   M *(No mistakes)*

23 A I heard about your new series
   B based on the lives of heroes'.
   C Please send me a sample copy.
   D *(No mistakes)*

24 J Your new series sounds exciting!
   K   Yours truly
   L   Victoria Hall
   M *(No mistakes)*

STOP

Level 12

74

SAY: **It is now time to stop. You have completed Test 4. Make sure that you have carefully filled in your answer spaces and have completely erased any stray marks. Then put your pencils down and close your books.**

After the test has been scored, review the questions and answer choices with students. If students are having difficulty, provide them with additional practice items.

Test 5: Language Expression

S1
- A Jim complains when he cannot
- B have friends over to visit. He says
- C he doesn't have nothing to do.
- D (No mistakes)

STOP

For questions 1–12, darken the circle for the line that has an error in the way words are used. If all the words are used correctly, darken the circle for *No mistakes*.

1
- A Saturday night we saw one of
- B the best movies ever made.
- C You ought to have seen it soon.
- D (No mistakes)

2
- J When I went shopping for new
- K school clothes, I got me two
- L pairs of pants and three shirts.
- M (No mistakes)

3
- A "One of the grapes are
- B squashed," said Dana. "Do I
- C have to eat it anyway?"
- D (No mistakes)

4
- J What is the most funniest joke
- K you know? Do you know the
- L one about the turtle and the car?
- M (No mistakes)

5
- A Allison done an excellent job
- B building her model of the solar
- C system for the science fair.
- D (No mistakes)

6
- J Ralph was thinking about his friend
- K Jamal on his birthday, so he sended
- L him a birthday card and a letter.
- M (No mistakes)

7
- A "Come over and pick up this
- B here sandwich you ordered!" called
- C the cook at the snack bar.
- D (No mistakes)

8
- J Ms. Porter and Mr. Sánchez is
- K the two most popular teachers
- L at school. They both teach English.
- M (No mistakes)

9
- A It is a good idea for people
- B who want to be baby-sitters
- C to take a first-aid course.
- D (No mistakes)

10
- J My aunt from Australia came
- K to visit last month. We were so
- L happily to see her that we cried.
- M (No mistakes)

11
- A I would have throwed out the bread
- B if I had seen that it was dry, but I
- C didn't realize it until I ate some.
- D (No mistakes)

12
- J For her birthday, Karima's
- K mother got the brand new
- L set of kitchen knifes she wanted.
- M (No mistakes)

GO ON

Level 12

75

Test 5: Language Expression

Allow 20 minutes for this test.

SAY: **Turn to Test 5, Language Expression, on page 75.**

Check to see that all students find Test 5.

SAY: **In this test you will use your language skills to find correct and incorrect language expression. Look at S1. Read the answer choices carefully. Then darken the circle for the correct answer.**

Allow students time to find and mark their answer.

SAY: **You should have darkened the circle for *C. Doesn't have nothing* is a double negative and shows incorrect usage.**

Check to see that all students have filled in the correct answer space. Ask students if they have any questions.

SAY: **Now you will finish the test on your own. Read the directions for each section carefully. Then do numbers 1 through 32 just as we did the sample. Darken the circle for each correct answer. When you come to the words *GO ON* at the bottom of a page, continue working on the next page. When you come to the word *STOP* at the bottom of page 78, put your pencils down. You have 20 minutes to complete the test. You may now begin.**

Allow students 20 minutes to find and mark their answers.

For questions 13–16, read the paragraph and the questions that follow. Then darken the circle for each correct answer. Darken the circle for *No change* if the answer is correct as it is.

[1] In early June a group of students found a hidden treasure. [2] It was a metal box buried over twenty years ago! [3] Inside the box were two hundred dollars. [4] Children have always looked for treasures but hardly ever find them. [5] The children were very excited, and they will spend some of the money. [6] Meanwhile, the owner of the box, who had forgotten where he had buried it, went to the police. [7] He asked that his money be returned. [8] Most of his treasure was returned, except for the part that was spent. [9] The kids weren't accused of stealing since the box had been buried.

13 Choose the best opening sentence to add to this paragraph.

A What would you do if you found a buried treasure?

B Some buried treasures are found even without maps.

C Some children would spend hundreds of dollars if they could.

D Money is safer put in a bank than buried in a box.

14 Which sentence does not belong in this paragraph?

J Sentence 2

K Sentence 4

L Sentence 5

M Sentence 7

15 Choose the best way to write the underlined part of sentence 5.

A are spending

B would spend

C spent

D *(No change)*

16 What is the best ending sentence for this paragraph?

J Those children will never forget finding a treasure!

K The owner of the metal box was thrilled to get the two hundred dollars back.

L Children should not dig for treasures that don't belong to them.

M The owner of the metal box knew it was silly to have buried that money!

For questions 17–22, darken the circle for the sentence or sentences that express the idea most clearly.

17 A Sherlock Holmes, a character and a famous detective, is well known.

B Well known, the character of Sherlock Holmes is a famous detective.

C A famous detective is well known. The character of Sherlock Holmes is.

D The well-known character of Sherlock Holmes is a famous detective.

18 J We peeked at the baby in the crib with the big, blue eyes.

K With big, blue eyes, we peeked at the baby in the crib.

L In the crib with the big, blue eyes was the baby we peeked at.

M We peeked in the crib at the baby who had big, blue eyes.

GO ON

Level 12

19 **A** In 1992, Bill Clinton was elected president of the United States.

    B Elected president of the United States, Bill Clinton was in 1992.

    C President Bill Clinton was elected in 1992 by the United States.

    D In 1992 elected, was Bill Clinton president of the United States.

20 **J** Before nightfall, the hikers were lost not reaching camp all night.

    K The hikers, lost all night in the woods, did not reach camp before nightfall.

    L Not reaching camp before nightfall, the hikers were lost all night in the woods.

    M The hikers were lost. Reaching camp before nightfall, they were not in the woods.

21 **A** In the vacant lot across the street, barking, Rafael heard a dog.

    B Barking in the vacant lot across the street, Rafael heard a dog.

    C A barking dog was heard by Rafael in the vacant lot across the street.

    D Rafael heard a dog barking in the vacant lot across the street.

22 **J** Proving they were the best team in the league, the Shepherds won 12–1.

    K They, the Shepherds, were in the league the best team, winning 12–1.

    L The Shepherds, the best team in the league, won 12–1, proving it.

    M Winning 12–1, the Shepherds in the league proved they were the best team.

For question 23, darken the circle for the paragraph that would be most appropriate at the end of a book report.

23 **A** Everyone should read this biography of Martin Luther King, Jr. It's pretty easy to read, and there are lots of pictures in it.

    B Martin Luther King, Jr., was one of the most important leaders America has ever known. This biography describes his struggles and his successes. More important, however, it shows that Dr. King's dream is still alive today because people still believe in the dream and work for it.

    C If you have to read a book about the civil rights movement, this one is okay. Martin Luther King, Jr., was an important leader. He helped lots of people. Every year, we celebrate his birthday in January with a national holiday.

    D I wish I could have met Dr. Martin Luther King, Jr., before he died. I'll bet you'll wish the same thing after you read this book about his life. You should go out and read it.

For questions 24–32, darken the circle for the word or words that best fit in the underlined part of the sentence. Darken the circle for *No change* if the sentence is correct as it is.

24 Being a native, Russell enjoys leading tours of the city.

J To be

K Is being

L Has been

M *(No change)*

25 My dad sent my mom a dozen roses if he loves her.

A because

B until

C then

D *(No change)*

26 As soon as we cast our lines, we have caught two big trout.

J caught

K have caughten

L catched

M *(No change)*

27 Nobody will buy cat food yesterday, and now we have none.

A is buying

B buys

C bought

D *(No change)*

28 Having learned to dance is very hard for some people.

J Learning

K Can be learning

L Learns

M *(No change)*

29 Beethoven will be one of my favorite composers.

A is

B should be

C are

D *(No change)*

30 Valerie won a writing competition last summer.

J will win

K winning

L wins

M *(No change)*

31 Every Saturday, to ride our bicycles, we go to the corner store.

A having ridden

B riding

C rides

D *(No change)*

32 Please turn off the lights since you walk out of the room.

J because

K when

L whereas

M *(No change)*

STOP

Level 12

78

SAY: **It is now time to stop. You have completed Test 5. Make sure that you have carefully filled in your answer spaces and have completely erased any stray marks. Then put your pencils down and close your books.**

After the test has been scored, review the questions and answer choices with students. If students are having difficulty, provide them with additional practice items.

S1 Which is the greatest common factor of 8 and 36?

- A 2
- B 4
- C 8
- D 42

STOP

For questions 1–31, darken the circle for the correct answer.

1 Which numeral has the greatest value?

6882	8362	6832	8623	6823

- A 2368
- B 6832
- C 8362
- D 8623

2 What is the value of the 4 in 23.46?

- J 4 tenths
- K 4 ones
- L 4 hundredths
- M 4 tens

3 What should replace the □ in the multiplication problem shown here?

- A 4
- B 5
- C 6
- D 7

```
      312
    × 46
    1872
   12□8
   14△52
```

4 What is another way to write forty-two thousandths?

- J 0.042
- K 0.42
- L 4.2
- M 42,000

5 Which is another way to write 6×10^5?

- A $6 \times \frac{5}{10}$
- B $6 \times 10 \times 10 \times 10 \times 10 \times 10$
- C $6 \times 10 \times 5$
- D $6 \times \frac{10}{5}$

6 Which numeral has the same value as $\frac{19}{4}$?

- J $1\frac{3}{4}$
- K $4\frac{1}{4}$
- L $4\frac{1}{2}$
- M $4\frac{3}{4}$

7 Which numeral will make this number sentence true?

$(5 \times \square) + 5 = 45$

- A 7
- B 8
- C 9
- D 10

GO ON

Level 12

Test 6: Math Concepts and Estimation

Allow 20 minutes for this test.

Distribute scratch paper to students. Tell them they may use the scratch paper to work all problems except numbers 28 through 31 on page 82. These are estimation problems that students should work in their heads.

SAY: **Turn to Test 6, Math Concepts and Estimation, on page 79.**

Check to see that all students find Test 6.

SAY: **In this test you will use your mathematics skills to solve problems. Look at S1. Read the question silently, then darken the circle for the correct answer.**

Allow students time to find and mark their answer.

SAY: **You should have darkened the circle for *B* because *4* is the greatest common factor of *8* and *36*.**

Check to see that all students have filled in the correct answer space. Ask students if they have any questions.

SAY: **Now you will finish the test on your own. Read the directions carefully. Do numbers 1 through 31 just as we did S1. Darken the circle for each correct answer. When you come to the words *GO ON* at the bottom of a page, continue working on the next page. When you come to the word *STOP* at the bottom of page 82, put your pencils down. You have 20 minutes to complete the test. You may now begin.**

Allow students 20 minutes to find and mark their answers.

8 Which numeral would replace the □ to make number sentence true?

$(4 + 5) + 9 = (9 + 4) + □$

J 0

K 4

L 5

M 9

9 What would replace the □ in the number sentence?

$73 - (45 - 6) + 10 = □$

A 32

B 42

C 44

D 112

10 What would replace the □ to make the fractions equivalent?

$\frac{16}{28} = \frac{□}{7}$

J 3

K 4

L 5

M 6

11 What would replace the □ to make the fractions equivalent?

$\frac{7}{12} = \frac{□}{36}$

A 3

B 10

C 21

D 28

12 Which unit of measurement is best to use to describe the height of a sixth-grade student?

J Inches

K Ounces

L Pounds

M Gallons

13 Which figure below is a parallelogram?

A   C

B   D

14 In the congruent figures shown here, which part of the second figure corresponds to $\overline{DE}$?

J $\overline{TV}$ L $\overline{VW}$

K $\overline{CD}$ M $\overline{SW}$

15 The figure below has $\frac{7}{9}$ of its area shaded. How much is <u>not</u> shaded?

A $\frac{2}{9}$

B $\frac{2}{10}$

C $\frac{2}{7}$

D $\frac{1}{9}$

GO ON

Level 12

80

16 What is a reasonable estimate of the width of a school locker?

J 12 inches

K 5 feet

L 512 centimeters

M 2 yards

17 Which angle shown here is equal to 90°?

 A

 C

 B

 D

18 What is another way to write 85 seconds?

J 8.5 minutes

K 0.85 minutes

L 1 minute 25 seconds

M 1.25 minutes

19 Which circle will fit within a 6-inch square and have the least amount of the square remain uncovered?

A 3 in.

C 12 in.

B 2 in.

D 6 in.

20 On a map of a cross-country ski trail, 1 inch represents 4 miles. **What is the length of the trail if the distance from the south end to the north end is 8 inches?**

J 3 miles

K 11 miles

L 20 miles

M 32 miles

21 Which set of numbers shown here has the greatest average (mean)?

A {2, 4, 8}

B {3, 5, 7}

C {1, 6, 9}

D {4, 5, 6}

22 For which of the following does a mean (average) not make sense?

J Number of lunches sold today

K Four science test scores

L Amount of snowfall each year

M Baby-sitting rates of sixth-grade students

23 On which letter is the spinner most likely to stop?

A A

B B

C C

D D

GO ON

24 The numbers in the two boxes shown here are formed by the same rule. **What number is missing?**

1, 3, 7, 15, 31, 63

0, 2, 6, 14, ☐, 62

J 28
K 30
L 31
M 32

25 What is the value of x if $\frac{x}{6} = 30$?

A 5 C 100
B 36 D 180

26 Which number line represents $x \le 4$?

J

K

L

M

27 What is the value of x if $\frac{x}{5} = 9$?

A 9 C 54
B 45 D 81

28 The closest estimate of the time remaining until departure is _____.

Departure time is 12:55 P.M.
Time now is 9:08 A.M.

J 3 hours L 5 hours
K 4 hours M 16 hours

29 The closest estimate of the cost of red apples is _____.

Red apples ?   Green apples $9.40   Total cost is $15.25.

A $6 C $60
B $25 D $180

30 The closest estimate of $23 \div 6\frac{3}{4}$ is _____.

J 3 L 5
K 4 M 17

31 The closest estimate of the cost of 28 folders is _____.

1 folder for 59¢

A $0.31 C $18.00
B $1.80 D $180.00

STOP
Level 12

82

Test 7: Math Problems

S1 The Harris family took a trip across the United States. They traveled about 1,573 miles by train and about 734 miles by bus. **Using these estimates, how many miles did the Harris family travel?**

A 839

B 2,307

C 2,370

D Not given

STOP

Directions: For questions 1–20, darken the circle for the correct answer. Darken the circle for Not given if the correct answer is not shown.

Use the table shown here to answer questions 1–3.

Park Admission Fees	
Adults	$18
Seniors	$9
Children (4–12 years)	$12
Children 3 and under free	
Three-day passes — $25 per person.	

1 How much would a group of 1 senior, 3 adults, and 6 children, ages 5–10, pay for admission?

A $125

B $130

C $135

D $140

2 How much would the same group pay if they each bought a three-day pass?

J $225

K $250

L $270

M $500

3 The Finnigan family had coupons for free admission for 2 children with 2 paid adults. Andy is 9, his brother Bryan is 7, and his sister Samantha is 3. **How much did Mr. and Mrs. Finnigan pay?**

A $36

B $60

C $72

D Not given

4 Meili started a new photo album. She has 34 pictures and plans to put 6 pictures on each page. **How many pages does Meili need?**

J 7   L 5

K 204   M 6

5 Trung had $16. He spent $7 bowling and $4 for lunch. At the card shop, he bought some packages of gift wrap and a birthday card with the rest of his money. The card cost more than the gift wrap. **What other information is needed to find out exactly how much Trung spent on the card?**

A How much the gift wrap cost

B How many sheets of gift wrap he bought

C The size of each sheet of gift wrap

D No additional information is needed

6 Diana is ordering pizza. Her choices include thin or thick crust, each with cheese and a choice of sausage or mushroom toppings. **How many different combinations of crust and toppings are possible?**

J 2

K 3

L 5

M 6

GO ON

Level 12

83

Test 7: Math Problems

Allow 20 minutes for this test.

Distribute scratch paper to students. Tell them to compute their answers on the scratch paper.

SAY: **Turn to Test 7, Math Problems, on page 83.**

Check to see that all students find Test 7.

SAY: **In this test you will use your mathematics skills to solve problems. Look at S1. Read the problem silently, then darken the circle for the correct answer.**

Allow students time to find and mark their answer.

SAY: **You should have darkened the circle for B because 1,573 + 734 = 2,307.**

Check to see that all students have filled in the correct answer space. Ask students if they have any questions.

SAY: **Now you will finish the test on your own. Read the directions carefully. Then do numbers 1 through 20 just as we did S1. Darken the circle for each correct answer. When you come to the words GO ON at the bottom of a page, continue working on the next page. When you come to the word STOP at the bottom of page 85, put your pencils down. You have 20 minutes to complete the test. You may now begin.**

Allow students 20 minutes to find and mark their answers.

7 Mona needed 3 cups of uncooked oatmeal for a recipe. **What should she do to find out how many times she needs to fill a $\frac{1}{2}$-cup measure?**

A Add $\frac{1}{2}$ and 3

B Multiply $\frac{1}{2}$ and 3

C Subtract $\frac{1}{2}$ from 3

D Divide 3 by $\frac{1}{2}$

8 Michiko helped pack individual boxes of cookies into carrying cases. Each carrying case holds 18 individual boxes. She packed 10 boxes of each of the 6 kinds of cookies available for sale. **How many individual boxes of cookies are left over?**

J 3   L 6

K 4   M 60

Use the graph shown here to answer questions 9 and 10.

After-School Activities

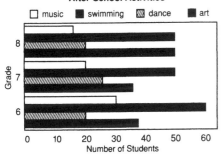

9 About how many students take dance lessons after school?

A 20   C 40

B 25   D 65

10 Which activity involves the greatest number of students in Grade 6?

J Music   L Dance

K Swimming   M Art

Use the graph shown here to answer questions 11–13.

11 During which week did the students turn in the most book reports?

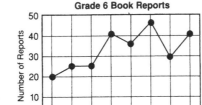

A Week 4

B Weeks 4 and 8

C Week 6

D Week 8

12 Which statement best describes the total number of book reports turned in between Week 1 and Week 4?

J The total fell steadily each week.

K The total rose sharply after 3 weeks.

L The total changed little.

M The total increased each month.

13 How many more book reports were done during weeks 5–8 than during weeks 1–4?

A 20   C 30

B 25   D 40

GO ON

Level 12

Use the table below to answer questions 14–17.

Mileage Chart

City	New Orleans	Atlanta	Denver
Chicago	919	708	1021
New York	1335	854	1794
Miami	860	663	2107
Dallas	517	822	784
Los Angeles	1858	2191	1031

14 How much farther is Dallas from Atlanta than Chicago from Atlanta?

J 114 miles   L 822 miles

K 708 miles   M 1530 miles

15 How far is New York from Denver?

A 854 miles   C 1794 miles

B 1021 miles   D 2107 miles

16 Which two cities are nearest to each other?

J Dallas and New Orleans

K Miami and Atlanta

L Los Angeles and Denver

M New York and Atlanta

17 Which city is farthest from Denver?

A Chicago   C Dallas

B Atlanta   D Miami

Use the graph below to answer questions 18–20.

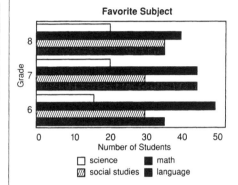

Favorite Subject

□ science ■ math
▨ social studies ■ language

18 Which subject ranks first with each class?

J Science

K Math

L Social studies

M Language

19 How many sixth-grade students like math class best?

A 15

B 50

C 30

D 35

20 Which grade has the most students?

J Grade 6

K Grade 7

L Grade 8

M Grades 6 and 8 have the same number.

STOP

Level 12

It is now time to stop. You have completed Test 7. Make sure that you have carefully filled in your answer spaces and have completely erased any stray marks. Then put your pencils down and close your books.

After the test has been scored, review the questions and answer choices with students. If students are having difficulty, provide them with additional practice.

Test 8: Math Computation

S1 $384 + 857 =$

- A 1131
- B 1231
- C 1241
- D N

STOP

S2 $92 - 34 =$

- J 38
- K 58
- L 68
- M N

STOP

For questions 1–10, darken the circle for the correct answer. Darken the circle for N if the answer is not given. Reduce answers that are fractions to lowest terms.

1 $7 + 182 + 96 =$

- A 275
- B 285
- C 385
- D N

2 $\frac{4}{6} + \frac{5}{6} =$

- J $\frac{1}{2}$
- K $\frac{20}{18}$
- L 1
- M N

3 $0.0606 + 0.709 =$

- A 0.1315
- B 0.7696
- C 7.696
- D N

4 $13 - \frac{5}{6} =$

- J $\frac{3}{4}$
- K $\frac{1}{4}$
- L 12
- M N

5 $583 - 391 =$

- A 182
- B 192
- C 292
- D N

6 $0.23 \times 0.09 =$

- J 0.0207
- K 0.2007
- L 0.207
- M N

7 $\frac{3}{5} \times 12$

- A 4
- B 9
- C 36
- D N

8 $7)\overline{5848}$

- J 763
- K 764
- L 765
- M N

9 $842 \div 34 =$

- A 24
- B 24 r26
- C 26
- D N

10 $43)\overline{761}$

- J 17r1
- K 17r3
- L 17r30
- M N

STOP

Level 12

86

Test 8: Math Computation

Allow 10 minutes for this test. Distribute scratch paper to students. Tell them to compute their answers on the scratch paper.

SAY: **Turn to Test 8, Math Computation, on page 86.**

Check to see that all students find Test 8.

SAY: **In this test you will use your mathematics skills to solve problems. Look at S1. You are asked to add 384 and 857. Work the problem. Then darken the circle for the correct answer. If the correct answer is not given, darken the circle for N.**

Allow students time to find and mark their answer.

SAY: **You should have darkened the circle for *C* because *384 + 857 = 1241*.**

Check to see that all students have filled in the correct answer space.

SAY: **Now look at S2. You are asked to subtract 34 from 92. Work the problem. Then darken the circle for the correct answer. If the correct answer is not given, darken the circle for N.**

Allow students time to find and mark their answer.

SAY: **You should have darkened the circle for *K* because *92 – 34 = 58*.**

Check to see that all students have filled in the correct answer space.

SAY: **Now you will finish the test on your own. Read the directions carefully. Then do questions 1 through 10 just as we did the samples. Darken the circle for each correct answer. If the correct answer is not given, darken the circle for N. When you come to the word *STOP* at the bottom of page 86, put your pencils down. You have 10 minutes to complete the test. You may now begin.**

Allow students 10 minutes to find and mark their answers.

SAY: **It is now time to stop. You have completed Test 8. Make sure that you have carefully filled in your answer spaces and have completely erased any stray marks. Then put your pencils down and close your books.**

After the test has been scored, review the questions and answer choices with students. If students are having difficulty, provide them with additional practice.

Test 9: Maps and Diagrams

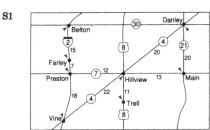

S1

Which city is located 22 miles from Vine?

A Preston

B Trell

C Hillview

D Farley

STOP

For questions 1–18, darken the circle for the correct answer.

Use the map shown here to answer questions 1–5.

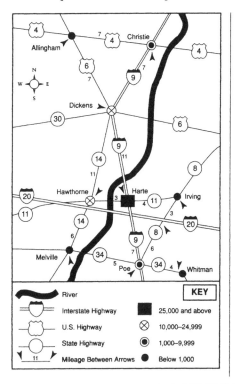

KEY

River		
Interstate Highway	■	25,000 and above
U.S. Highway	⊗	10,000–24,999
State Highway	⊙	1,000–9,999
Mileage Between Arrows	●	Below 1,000

1 Which city is located at the intersection of highways 9 and 34?

A Whitman   C Melville

B Poe   D Hawthorne

2 Which of these might be the population of Dickens?

J 783   L 18,245

K 5,437   M 31,622

3 Which highways probably do not have a bridge over the river?

A 30 and 14   C 6 and 34

B 9 and 11   D 20 and 4

4 What is the mileage between Dickens and Christie by the shortest route?

J 7 miles   L 11 miles

K 9 miles   M 14 miles

5 If Jan Stewart walks 4 miles west from Irving, how many more miles will she have to walk to get to Hawthorne?

A 2 miles   C 6 miles

B 3 miles   D 11 miles

GO ON

Level 12

87

Test 9: Maps and Diagrams

Allow 20 minutes for this test.

SAY: **Turn to Test 9, Maps and Diagrams, on page 87.**

Check to see that all students find Test 9.

SAY: **In this test you will use your study skills to interpret information in visual materials. Look at S1. Study the map carefully. Read the question silently, then darken the circle for the correct answer.**

Allow students time to find and mark their answer.

SAY: **You should have darkened the circle for *C* because the map shows that *Hillview* is located 22 miles from Vine.**

Check to see that all students have filled in the correct answer space. Ask students if they have any questions.

SAY: **Now you will finish the test on your own. Read the directions carefully. Study the visual materials. Then do questions 1 through 18 just as we did the S1. Darken the circle for each correct answer. When you come to the words *GO ON* at the bottom of a page, continue working on the next page. When you come to the word *STOP* at the bottom of page 89, put your pencils down. You have 20 minutes to complete the test. You may now begin.**

Allow students 20 minutes to find and mark their answers.

The two maps below show an imaginary country made up of four states. Use the maps to answer questions 6–11.

Political/Physical Map Key

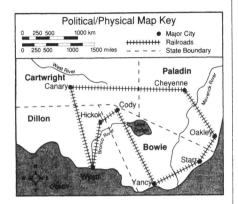

Products/Resources Key

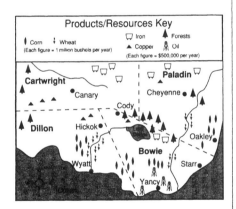

6 What is the shortest distance by railroad from Cody to Yancy?

J 525 miles

K 800 miles

L 1000 miles

M 1700 miles

7 If a train was traveling from Yancy to Starr, in which direction would it be going?

A Northeast

B Southeast

C Northwest

D Southwest

8 What is the value of copper produced in Dillon each year?

J $500,000

K $1,000,000

L $1,500,000

M $2,000,000

9 Which city is shown in this picture?

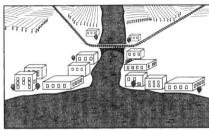

A Starr   C Cody

B Yancy   D Wyatt

10 What product is most likely shipped out of Oakley by railroad?

J Copper   L Corn

K Iron   M Oil

11 What is most likely a major industry in Yancy?

A Food canning

B Fish processing

C Oil refining

D Steel manufacturing

GO ON

Level 12

88

Use the diagram shown here to answer questions 12–14.

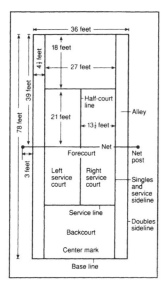

12 How long is a tennis court?

J 27 feet L 39 feet

K 36 feet M 78 feet

13 How many feet is the net from the service line?

A 18 feet C 27 feet

B 21 feet D 39 feet

14 Which of the following is an accurate statement?

J The forecourt is longer than the backcourt.

K The backcourt is longer than the forecourt.

L The distance from the singles sideline to the doubles sideline is 3 feet.

M The backcourt is between the net and the service line.

Use the table shown here to answer questions 15–18.

County Fair Events					
	11:00 12:00	1:00	2:00	3:00	
FRI	Judging of 4-H craft projects	Foot races — — — — — — →			
		Toddlers	4–5 year olds	6–8 year olds	
SAT	Pet parade	Foot races — — — — — — →			
	Judging of 4-H farming projects	9–10 year olds	11–12 year olds	13–14 year olds	
			Teddy bear picnic		
SUN	Baby contest	Crowning of 4-H king and queen	Marching band contest		
	Judging of 4-H livestock projects				

15 Which event could people attend on Friday morning?

A Judging of 4-H livestock projects

B Teddy bear picnic

C Baby contest

D Judging of 4-H craft projects

16 How many events are scheduled for Saturday?

J 2 L 6

K 5 M 7

17 If eleven-year-old Yuko and twelve-year-old Lupe entered the foot races, when would their race begin?

A Friday at 1:00 P.M.

B Saturday at 1:00 P.M.

C Saturday at 2:00 P.M.

D Saturday at 3:00 P.M.

18 Kyle raised a pig named Rufus for a 4-H project and entered Rufus in the fair. When would Kyle learn whether Rufus won a prize?

J By 11:00 A.M. Friday

K By 2:00 P.M. Friday

L After 3:00 P.M. Saturday

M By 1:00 P.M. Sunday

STOP

Level 12

89

S1 Which of these would you find in an atlas?

A A discussion of the cultural groups in Chile

B A description of the government of Chile

C The names of the mountains found in Chile

D A description of the economy of Chile

STOP

For questions 1–22, darken the circle for the correct answer.

Use the index to answer questions 1–8.

INDEX

Aquariums, 45–57

Birds, cages, 78–83; care, 63–68; food, 59–61; types of, 69–75; *See also* First Aid

Cages, for small animals, 91; for birds, 78–83; care, cleaning, and repair, 84–90

Cats, breeds, 123–129; diet, 132; diseases, 142–146; exercise, 134; grooming, 138; *See also* First Aid

Dogs, breeds, 93–101; diet, 103; diseases, 117–119; exercise, 105–108; grooming, 110; guard dogs, 121; obedience training, 112–114; *See also* First Aid

First aid, birds, 76; cats, 140; dogs, 115

Fish, types, 35–40; care and feeding, 41

Pets, types, 2–23; selecting a pet, 24–34

1 Which page would most likely have information about diseases dogs get through fleas?

A 24   C 117

B 112   D 142

2 Which page might explain how to fix the bars on a parrot's cage?

J 59   L 69

K 63   M 84

3 Which page might have information about caring for a parrot that has a broken wing?

A 40   C 78

B 76   D 115

4 Which page might explain how to care for tropical fish?

J 41   L 100

K 69   M 134

5 Which page might tell how to stop a dog from chewing furniture?

A 63   C 112

B 105   D 117

6 Which page might tell which pet would be best for people who live in apartments?

J 24   L 105

K 35   M 142

7 Which page might explain how to set up a cage for hamsters?

A 35   C 84

B 78   D 91

8 Which page might have information about setting up an aquarium for tropical fish?

J 35   L 45

K 41   M 84

GO ON

Level 12

Test 10: Reference Materials

Allow 20 minutes for this test.

SAY: **Turn to Test 10, Reference Materials, on page 90.**

Check to see that all students find Test 10.

SAY: **In this test you will use your study skills to identify reference sources and to locate and interpret information in them. Look at S1. Read the question silently, then darken the circle for the correct answer.**

Allow students time to find and mark their answer.

SAY: **You should have darkened the circle for *C* because an atlas would show the mountains in Chile.**

Check to see that all students have filled in the correct answer space. Ask students if they have any questions.

SAY: **Now you will finish the test on your own. Read the directions carefully. Then do numbers 1 through 22 just as we did S1. Darken the circle for each correct answer. When you come to the words *GO ON* at the bottom of a page, continue working on the next page. When you come to the word *STOP* at the bottom of page 92, put your pencils down. You have 20 minutes to complete the test. You may now begin.**

Allow students 20 minutes to find and mark their answers.

Use the dictionary and the pronunciation key to answer questions 9–11.

---

gar•ret (**gar'** it) *n.* The top floor or room of a house, directly below the roof; the attic.

ga•zette (gə **zet'**) *n.* **1.** A newspaper or similar periodical. **2.** Any official publication as of a government or institution.

gen•er•ate (**jen'** ər rāt) *v.* To produce or cause to be.

glim•mer (**glim'** ər) *n.* **1.** A dim, unsteady light. **2.** A hint or sign. —*v.* To shine with dim light; flicker.

grad•u•al (**graj'** ü əl) *adj.* **1.** Moving, changing, or happening slowly or by degrees. **2.** Not steep or abrupt.

gram•mat•i•cal (grə **mat'** i kəl) *adj.* **1.** Of or relating to grammar. Imposing or impressive. **2.** Following the rules of grammar.

---

1. Pronunciation Key

a	at	o	hot	u̇	pull
ā	ape	ō	old	û	turn
ä	far	ô	song	ch	chin
â	care	ô	fork	ng	sing
e	end	oi	oil	sh	shop
e	me	ou	out	th	thin
i	it	u	up	t̲h̲	this
ī	ice	ū	use	hw	in white
î	pierce	ü	rule	zh	in treasure

The ə symbol stands for the unstressed vowel heard in about, taken, pencil, lemon, and circus.

2. Abbreviations: *n.*, noun; *v.*, verb; *adj.* adjective; *pl.*, plural.

---

9 When *-ly* is added, which word becomes an adverb?

A garret C gradual

B glimmer D generate

10 Which word could be used to describe a place in a house that can be used to store things?

J garret L generate

K gazette M glimmer

11 Which syllable of *grammatical* is accented?

A The first

B The second

C The third

D The fourth

Use the dictionary guide words shown here to answer questions 12–14.

buckskin / bug	98
buggy / bulletin	99
bullfight / bunny	100
Bunsen burner / burr	101
burro / bustle	102

12 On which page would you find the word *budget?*

J 98 L 100

K 99 M 101

13 On which page would you find the word *bungalow?*

A 98 C 102

B 100 D 103

14 On which page would you find the word *bunting?*

J 98 L 101

K 99 M 103

GO ON

Use the card from the library card catalog to answer questions 15–17.

GERMAN PLANES

722.43   Barker, Fredereich

German Planes of World War II /
by Fredereich Barker;
photographs by Owen James.
New York City: Military Press, 1989.
163p. : illus. ; 27 cm.

1. German Planes   2. World War II.
I. Title.

---

15   **What is the title of this book?**

A   German Planes of World War II

B   Fredereich Barker

C   World War II

D   Military Press

16   **Which number will help you find this book in the library?**

J   1989   L   163

K   722.43   M   27

17   **What key word does the card tell you to use to find other information about World War II?**

A   Germany

B   World War II

C   Military Press

D   History

18   **Which of these would show you how to correctly divide the word** *continent* **at the end of a line?**

J   An atlas

K   A dictionary

L   A geography book

M   An encyclopedia

19   **In which section of the library would you find sports magazines?**

A   Fiction

B   Reference

C   Nonfiction

D   Periodicals

20   **Which key term would you use to find out about the kinds of plants and animals that live on the steppes of southern Ukraine and central Asia?**

J   Asia

K   Steppes

L   Plants

M   Animals

21   **Which key term would you use to find information about Wrigley Field, the home of the Chicago Cubs baseball team?**

A   Parks

B   Chicago

C   Wrigley Field

D   Baseball

22   Nomadic people of North Africa use the camel for transportation in the desert. **Which key term would you use to find information about the eating habits of camels?**

J   Eating habits

K   Camels

L   North Africa

M   Deserts

STOP
Level 12

92

SAY: **It is now time to stop. You have completed Test 10. Make sure that you have carefully filled in your answer spaces and have completely erased any stray marks. Then put your pencils down and close your books.**

After the test has been scored, review the question and answer choices with students. If students are having difficulty, provide them with additional practice.